Memoirs of a Marine Dawg:

From Rose Bowl to Pacific Theater

by Curtis Beall

Indigo Custom Publishing, LLC

Publisher	Henry S. Beers
Associate Publisher	Richard J. Hutto
Executive Vice President	Robert G. Aldrich
Chief Operations Manager	Gary G. Pulliam
Editor-in-Chief	Joni Woolf
Art Director/Designer	Julianne Gleaton
Designer	Daniel Emerson
Director of Marketing and Public Relations	Mary D. Robinson

Printed in U.S.A.

Library of Congress Control Nmber: 2006932424

ISBN: (10 Digit) 1-934144-01-0 ISBN: (13 Digit) 978-1-934144-01-5

Indigo Custom Publishing, LLC books are available at quantity discounts with bulk purchase for educational, business, or sales promotional use.

For information, please write to:
Indigo Custom Publishing, LLC • SunTrust Bank Building • 435 Second St. • Suite 320 • Macon, GA 31201, or call toll free 866-311-9578.

Cover image: Curtis Beall, UGA VI, and Beall's granddaughter, Lisa Love. Lisa is a former member of the UGA Redcoat Band's Flagline.

11-11-06

BOB:

THANKS FOR PLANNING OUR MARINE BREAKFAST EVERY YEAR. SOMETIMES IT EVEN TAKES A TECH MAN TO GET THE JOB DONE.

HOPE YOU ENJOY THE BOOK.

[illegible signature]

DEDICATION

This book is dedicated to my family and to the past, present, and future cheerleaders and their coaches at UGA. The net proceeds from the sale of this book will be donated to "Cheers," the Booster Club for the University's cheerleaders.

CONTENTS

Memoirs of a Marine Dawg:
From Rose Bowl to Pacific Theater

ACKNOWLEDGEMENTS

It is indeed my privilege to express my gratitude to those who have made the publication of this book possible.

First, I deeply appreciate the work of Faye Price, East Laurens High School English Department Chairman. Not only was she my editor, but also she was a constant source of encouragement in this effort.

I am truly grateful to my daughter, Anita Welborn, whose unique ability to decode my penmanship and transfer my ideas to the computer resulted in a readable manuscript for others to enjoy.

In addition, I sincerely appreciate the special assistance and diligent support of my niece, Kathy Sweat.

Finally, I am appreciative of Indigo Custom Publishing's staff's enthusiastic cooperation in publishing my two books – my first and last.

INTRODUCTION

According to legendary Army general, Douglas McArthur, in his 1951 speech before a joint session of Congress, "Old soldiers never die; they just fade away."

Well, Curtis Beall was never a soldier. He was a Marine, and there is no evidence that he is "fading away." In his eighth decade, he has many stories to tell as he continues to live a life of work, pleasure, and support for his alma mater, the University of Georgia.

In this delightful retrospective, Beall tells those stories with historical accuracy and colorful anecdotes. Tales from his early life in Brewton, Georgia, are also stories of the coming-of-age of the modern South. His eye for detail and his remarkable memory color these reminiscences with realistic and remarkable characters—boys he grew up with, teachers who inspired him, and relatives who brought him up with a strict set of values that have influenced him throughout his life.

He tells with humor and clarity about his days at UGA, where he found the girl of his dreams—June Clarke—his bride of sixty years. A campus leader throughout his university career, Beall was known on campus for his involvement in a variety of UGA activities, including his reputation as a cheerleader. In fact, Curtis Beall is the oldest, active, living, male, UGA cheerleader, and he and his family have attended Bulldog games throughout the years, revisiting the campus and renewing acquaintances with each new season.

Leaving the university before graduation to enter active duty in the U.S. Marines during World War II, Beall found himself in the Pacific Theater toward the end of the war. A leader of men in the war effort, Beall was in Okinawa when the Japanese surrendered, and his tales add to the lore of that momentous time in American history.

His subsequent careers are the stuff of legend: He and his bride came to Brewton to begin their married life, and soon he was managing the Federal Land Bank, a position for which he was uniquely qualified. Beall knew farming, and he knew farmers; some of his stories will have readers smiling, as he recounts humorous and unusual events from that time.

Careers of entrepreneurship have been a large part of Beall's life for the past thirty years, as he and his family have enjoyed Christmas tree farming, catfish farming, and wine-making. A man of boundless energy, Beall has operated all these businesses with an eye on the future, beginning and ending ventures as necessary and adjusting to what the times have demanded.

Through it all, the girl of his dreams has been at his side, cheering him on, as together they have raised a family and now enjoy visits with extended family both at home and at the University on home-game week-ends. On Homecoming weekend, wearing his sixty-four year old cheerleading sweater, Beall is one of the alumni cheerleader float participants in the parade through downtown Athens. An enthusiastic supporter of the Georgia cheerleading squad, Beall intends to donate the net proceeds from this book to "Cheers," the Booster Club, to support cheerleaders as they warm up the crowds and cheer the Bulldogs on to victory.

Curtis Beall is a lucky man. He knows how to look backward, and he knows how to look forward. Just around the corner is another adventure waiting for him. No doubt he'll find it with June by his side, as they continue life's exciting journey, living every day to the fullest and giving thanks for all that was—and is to come.

GROWING UP IN A SMALL TOWN

GROWING UP IN A SMALL TOWN

Chapter 1

I was born on September 23, 1922, in Claxton's Hospital on Bellevue Avenue in Dublin, Georgia. Years later, when Claxton's Hospital was sold, it became Mr. Bill Lovett's residence and private home. After a few days in the hospital, I became a new resident of the small town of Brewton. The original name of the town was Dodo, pronounced Dough-Dough, located about one-half mile from the present site. When the Wrightsville and Tennille Railroad was built, one of its stations was near Bruton Creek. As a result, the town moved to be near the railroad, and the name and spelling were changed to Brewton.

Not long after the W & T Railroad was constructed, a second railroad, the Brewton and Pinora railroad, was started and terminated there. Thus, the town had two railroads connecting it to all parts of the county and many parts of the state. The population increased because Brewton was the trading center for an area of six to eight miles. The town was chartered in 1889, flourished, and prospered. The population in 1900 was 292 residents, 214 in 1910, 247 in 1920, 151 in 1930, and 100 in 1990. The town thrived with the popularity of the railroad, but it died a corporate death with the railroad's decline and the arrival of the boll weevil in the 1920s.

W & T Railroad and B & P Railroad Highway

Downtown Brewton consisted of various businesses, which made it somewhat unique. One of the businesses was Dr. C.G. Moye's drug store, grocery store, and doctor's office. This was a brick flat-roofed pentagon-shaped building with bars on the windows. There were groceries on one side of the store, medicine in two-gallon brown jugs on the other side, and the doctor's office in the back.

Another business was The Yellow Dog, located next to Dr. Moye's store. This building was given its name by one of the more infamous town residents. The owner sold groceries, hamburgers, fish, seafood, hot dogs, and beer on the side.

There were several department stores and grocery stores owned by I.E.Thigpen, Ben Maddox, Dessie Maddox, Milton Thigpen, John Curl, and the Beall brothers (Hartwell and M.F.). The stores and major businesses were clustered along the railroad. The stores were built of unpainted heart pine wood with sloped tin roofs that usually protruded in front of the store. There was generally a loafer's bench where the local people gathered to chat; occasionally there was a porch for the same purpose. The floors were constructed of green wood, which shrank and left large cracks. These cracks provided the men of the town a favorite pastime, "pitchin' pennies." In this "pitchin' pennies" game, the person who pitched a penny closest to the crack won, while the person whose penny landed farthest away from the crack bought the other men a Coke. Once a year, the little boys in town were allowed to go under the buildings to collect the pennies. Sometimes during cotton-picking season, the boys even had enough money of their own to participate in this degenerate pastime. The department stores sold a variety of groceries, coffins, millinery, buggies, shirts, trousers, ladies' wear, shoes, candy, ice, and ice cream. The Post Office was located in one of the rear rooms of Beall Brothers. After 1943, Beall's Store was the only business in Brewton. After sixty-one years of business, Beall's Store closed its doors in September 1994.

The town bank was Farmers and Merchants Bank, which was a brick flat-roofed building with large front windows and double glass-paneled doors. The bank moved into the nearby town of Dublin in 1938 after a robbery right out of *Bonnie & Clyde* in 1934 and a series of minor burglaries in the following years. From 1942 – 1960, the Post Office was located in this building.

Also, there were a barber shop, a blacksmith shop, where a customer could have horses shoed or buy any kind of ironwork, a sawmill, a gristmill, a cotton warehouse, a cotton gin, and a Delco Light Plant owned by the city. The Delco Light Plant generated electricity before the Rural Electric Association was established and contained twenty to twenty-four batteries. Each battery was larger than a car battery. When the plant ran, it stored electrical current in the batteries. The three or four streetlights in town and several stores received their power from the Delco Light Plant.

The railroad depot had an inclined platform that ran between the tracks of the two railroads. Also, there were Section Houses and the Section Foreman's House. Because the railroad maintenance crews were responsible for the maintenance of a section of the track, it was convenient for the foreman and his crew of laborers to live near the railroad. The foreman and his family lived in a house along the railroad, and his crew of laborers and their families lived in one-room shanties down the track from the foreman's house.

Court House and Voting Precient

The jail, or calaboose, was a small wooden building with barred windows about the size of standard windowpanes and two cells. The jail was located to the rear of the Beall Brothers' store.

The courthouse was a wooden building with a small front porch. The townspeople voted in this building, and the young boys enjoyed gathering on its front porch. The present structure, located on the same site, is concrete block, but its size and style resemble the original structure.

Brewton Cemetery

The city well was a hand pump and a trough for watering horses and mules that pulled people's wagons to town on Saturday afternoons. When Brewton was incorporated in the 1920s and 1930s, low brick walls were put around all the main streets to hold the soil in place. The cemetery was located just across the intersection of the railroad tracks. Many of the names mentioned in this book have been placed on headstones in the Brewton Cemetery. Two white churches and two black churches were all wooden structures with steeples; some contained functional church bells. Outhouses to be used for emergencies were located in the woods behind the church buildings. There were two restaurants and a school. The original school was a wooden structure on Peachtree Street. A new brick school that consolidated four school districts was built in 1922. When the new brick school was built further down Peachtree, the original school was then used for a basketball court.

Residential Area

The original houses of the Depression were one-story structures with large windows on all sides of the house, chimneys, and real front porches suitable for rocking chairs and porch swings. These houses had tin roofs, and some gables even displayed gingerbread-type woodwork and fancy shingle designs.

Brewton School
1928

There were two boarding houses in Brewton in the 1930s: the Blankenship Boarding House and the Brantley Boarding House. These housed the single teachers who were required to live in their own school districts, other professionals, and occasional travelers. When freight trains remained overnight in Brewton, their crews divided into groups to spend the night in these boarding houses. Also, these two boarding houses served delicious meals to local people daily.

Outbuildings and Farm Buildings

Behind some of the residences were outbuildings. The buildings in these pictures are located presently behind the M.F. Beall home in Brewton. They were built of wood, unpainted with tin roofs, and were used as multi-purpose buildings.

The buggy house, where buggies were parked, had a corncrib in the middle room and a side room for storing gasoline engines. The building on the right of the buggy house was another storage house for farm implements.

The storage house building was located close to the main house and was used for storing old clothes and memorabilia. Originally, it did not have the shelters on each side.

The well house sheltered the family's water supply and was the storage place for the owner's personal Delco light plant. This was a 32Volt Delco system that ran one or two hours per day, two to three times a week to keep the batteries charged. This Delco light plant

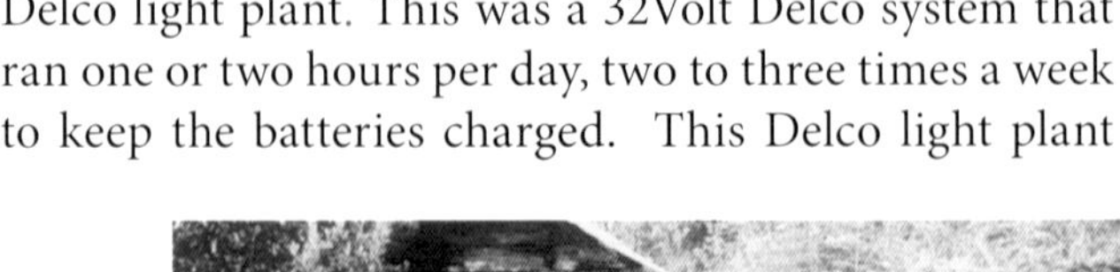

Barn and Shed

Corn Crib, Barn and Buggy House

provided a convenience for the family. Lights hung from a drop cord in the ceiling and had an on/off switch attached to the light socket. In the living room or dining room, a fancier pull string for the light was used. Mr. Hodges Boatwright, the brick mason, and M. F. Beall Sr., my father and owner, signed this particular well, dated March 20, 1929.

Corn for livestock, along with cottonseed, was stored in the corn crib, also called the cotton seed house. Many a rainy day, I crawled up into this cottonseed house, burrowed down in the cottonseed, and listened to the sound of rain on the tin roof. In the wintertime, there was no warmer place for me to be than burrowed down in the middle of the cottonseed.

Well House

Cane syrup was made in the syrup kettle boiler from locally grown sugar cane, which most all farmers grew. This was an example of how people during this era produced most of what they ate. The pig and cow chute was used to run pigs and cows onto the truck on the way to the market. The stable for mules was where the mules that pulled the wagons and helped on the farm were housed. These mules pulled plows, scooter stocks, cultivators, guano distributors, planters, and other farming implements. Mules were fed at lunch every day and at night.

Houses of Sharecroppers and Farmhands

Away from town was the farm. Most of the farm was pasture for livestock or crop land. Sharecroppers and farmhands generally lived in shotgun houses, which were small, unpainted wooden structures with tin roofs, front porches, and shuttered windows with no indoor plumbing. They usually had one fireplace in the middle of the house. One family lived in the house and paid no rent. The sharecropper and landowner agreed on how much the sharecropper would receive each month to pay for food and clothes. The landowner let him work a small acreage and furnished the sharecropper with seed, fertilizer, mules, and implements. After harvest, the sharecropper paid back what he owed the landowner. If there was anything remaining, they divided it on a fifty-fifty basis.

According to an article written by Dr. John C. Belcher and published in the *Dublin Courier Herald* in 1989, "Many small towns of Georgia have lost population and their economic foundations, but Brewton has been harder hit than most. Local residents think the reasons are obvious. Highway 80, a short distance to the south, and Highway 319, nearby to the north, were paved years ago, leaving Brewton on a dirt road in between; so it was bypassed as people went elsewhere to trade. Today, it is at the intersection of paved roads that receive only local traffic; so functionally it is still being bypassed by a world that does not know it even exists."

Sharecropper House

Although Brewton was a small town, fortunately several boys near my age and I grew up together. Their names and nicknames are as follows: Curtis Beall, Coot; Alton Jordan, Red; Keiver Jordan, Keive; Duggan Moye, Doc; Victor Moye, Vic; Charles Thompkins, Litt; John L. Tyre, Gus; and William Craig Tyre, Pete.

We grew up during the Great Depression, but we were thankful for adequate food, fuel, clothing, and shelter. We learned the true value of the necessities of life and did not have the government informing us frequently that we were poor if we did not have a family income of "X" number of dollars annually. We were all poor and had a somewhat primitive lifestyle compared to today's standard of living.

All the families had big gardens and raised their own food. My father was a farmer, as well as a merchant, and made enough home cured meat, syrup, flour, and meal to supply not only our family, but also the sharecroppers on the farms. Every member of the family had the responsibility of certain jobs, and these jobs were completed without question. At an early age, we learned the value of hard work. One of my jobs was to locate the milk cows every afternoon, put them in the cow lot, feed them dry feed such as cotton seed meal and hulls, and lock the cows in their stables for milking the following morning. There was a black lady named Jessie Reese, who did the milking every morning, helped my mother with the household chores, and was almost like a member of the family. She worked with our family from 1920 until 1955, when she was not able to work any longer.

We did not have electricity until about 1938, when my father purchased a Delco light plant. We used the Delco light plant until the Rural Electric Cooperatives organized and ran electric lines to the rural areas. With the coming of electricity, we were able to install a pressure pump on our dug well. Electricity enabled us to have indoor plumbing, radios, and electric lights.

Until we were ten or eleven years old, we wore either overalls and under shorts or short pants in the spring and summer. We seldom wore shoes unless we were attending Sunday School and church. Normally, we had a slingshot in our hip pockets and were fairly skilled at killing birds, rabbits, and other types of small wildlife. When I was twelve years old, my father sat me down and showed me how to load, aim, and shoot a 22 rifle and 20-gauge pump shotgun. He also informed me about the danger of both weapons. He cautioned me never to aim a gun at anything I did not intend to kill. To this day, I still follow my father's advice.

H. H. Beall House

Even though we worked hard on the farm or on other chores, our parents gave us time to grow up as boys and to hunt and fish with the other boys. Brewton Creek was about 150 yards from our house and provided the boys in town with a place to fish and swim. In the daytime, we fished with hand poles or reels or hand fished if the fish were not biting. Hand fishing was a method of fishing where we took off our clothes, usually put them under the old wooden Brewton Creek Bridge, got into the water, and started feeling under logs and in the moss along the creek bank to find a fish. When we felt a fish, we grabbed it with both hands and threw it onto the bank. Sometimes, we hand fished down one side of the creek a couple of miles, fished down the other side, and returned to our starting point. We also used set hooks in early spring to catch catfish. We caught mudpuppies, or spring lizards, under logs in wet places along the creek, and cut them into small pieces to bait the set hook. The set hook was tied on a cord about three feet long with a lead sinker onto a five-foot pole. We stuck the opposite end of the pole in the dirt along the creek with the bait about one foot in the water. We also fished at night with carbide lights or gas lanterns; consequently, the light blinded the fish. We waded into the water, placed the barrel of a 22 rifle into the water, and shot under the fish. The concussion killed the fish without damaging the meat. There were times we set out gill nets or seined the creek if we wanted the fish for a fish fry. If one method did not work, we tried another method until we caught enough fish.

The creek also provided us with a place to take a bath in the spring and summer prior to the time electricity became available and we had indoor bathrooms. The creek, which was supplied with water from several springs, provided us with a nice swimming hole, known as the Blue Hole. Every summer we cut a log about twelve inches in diameter and about fifteen feet long, placed it across the creek at the head of the Blue Hole, and drove stobs down by the side of the log to keep it in place. When the current became swift from winter rains, the swift moving water over the log increased the depth of the swimming hole and washed out any leaves or trash. The creek banks around the Blue Hole were blue mud, which we used to make bowls and pitchers.

Brewton School, like most rural schools at the time, was not accredited. In 1934, Brewton School was only in session for four months because the children picked cotton until the crop was gathered. Consequently, my parents sent my brother and me to school in Dublin, which had accredited schools. I became a student at Johnson Street Grammar School in 1928. The building was a two story wooden structure with the chapel on the second floor. There was a small emergency door on the back wall that opened onto a sheet metal sliding board to the ground. This door and sliding board served as the fire escape. A few of us enjoyed sliding on the sliding board after school was dismissed and the teachers had left the building. We attended chapel at least twice weekly. We lined up single file in our homeroom and marched to the chapel to one of Sousa's marches, played on a Victrola located in the central part of the building. The chapel program always started with one of the teachers reading a few verses of scripture and a prayer. Then we sang patriotic songs, read poems, and listened to announcements. After the announcements, we marched back to our homeroom.

My grandmother lived in an apartment about one-half block from the school. At lunchtime, I ran to her apartment and had lunch with her. I did this until I was in the third grade and one of the teachers saw me leave the campus. After that, my lunch arrangement was terminated, so my grandmother brought my lunch to the campus every day. We enjoyed talking to each other until I finished lunch. After she returned to her apartment, I played with the other students. We followed this routine until I completed the sixth grade.

When I was in the second grade, a contest was conducted to determine the healthiest boy and girl in the school system. I was selected to represent the boys, and a girl was selected from Calhoun Street School. Dr. Ovid Cheek, the Laurens County Health doctor, and two of the school principals were members of the selection committee. May Day, the first day of the month, was a special day. The students always looked forward to the celebration. A twelve-foot-high May Pole was fixed in the ground, and some of the students carrying a two-inch ribbon attached to the top of the pole marched in and out around the pole until the ribbon gave out. Various contests included sack races, 100-yard dashes, high jumps, broad jumps, and the parade. The healthiest girl and I rode on a float in the downtown parade. The float was a Model T Ford truck with a flatbed body covered with artificial grass. The artificial grass appeared to be the same as that used during graveside services by funeral homes today. The parade began at the Laurens County Courthouse, traveled west on Jackson Street, which was cobblestone or brick, to the library, which is presently the Museum. After a left turn on Church Street, the parade stopped so that the driver of our Model T truck could put more water in the radiator, which had run hot. He got the water from the elevated water trough directly across the street from the library. After that interruption, the parade turned left on Academy, continued back to Jackson Street, and returned to the starting point. I wore a white suit made by my mother's friend, a black cardboard top hat, and black shoes that were too small. I was very anxious to complete the parade so that I could get those shoes off.

My brother and I rode to school in an old model Chevrolet. My brother was the driver until he finished high school in 1935. Normally, there were nine or ten people riding to and from school with us because other families were eager for their children to attend an accredited school also. Frequently, the doors on the car did not lock when closed, so we carried a few pieces of haywire to wrap around the door to prevent anyone from falling out of the car.

When I was in the fourth grade, the principal and fourth grade teacher was Mrs. W.W. Ward. She introduced the multiplication tables and gave her students two weeks to learn the tables well enough to recite them from memory in front of the class. All the students in the class except three of us boys, who were too busy playing marbles to study, met the deadline. Although she gave us one additional day to learn the tables, we still thought playing marbles was more important. When she called on the three of us to recite the multiplication tables the following day, we failed to recite the tables. Consequently, as we leaned over a desk, she gave us three licks with a paddle in front of the class. That night, before I went to bed, I learned my multiplication tables by the light in the fireplace and recited them correctly the next day.

We enjoyed playing tops and marbles for keeps at school recess, at home in the afternoons, and on weekends. Frequently, in the summertime, we played "hole marbles for knucks." The older men played with us. Although we were young boys, the older men took no pity on us. Three holes about the size of a cup and ten feet apart in a straight line were dug in the ground, and another hole was dug at a right angle ten feet from the last hole. The first hole was called "home" and the starting point for each player. The object was to ring each hole, return toward home, and then return to the last hole. If the first player's marble hit the second player's marble, the second player was considered "dead" and had to start all over again. The last player to complete the game was the loser, and all the other players would shoot the loser's knuckles according to the number of times they had indicated before the game started. The loser balled his fist up and placed it on the ground next to one of the holes. If the shooter's marble landed in the hole after shooting the loser's knuckle, the loser shot that person's knuckle. Normally, the game was ten knuckles for each winner. If there were five players in the game, the loser had his knuckles hit forty times. Usually, the winners hit the same knuckle in the same place. As a result of this game, most of us became very skilled at playing marbles.

We made many of our toys. One of our favorites was a round metal band about three-fourths inches wide and ten inches in diameter. It was rolled with a stiff piece of wire about three feet long; one end was bent in the shape of an "L" to guide the metal wheel. The wheel band had been used to tighten and hold the hub on wagons and buggies that had wooden spokes. Another favorite activity was to make our own wagons and carts which were used for different purposes. I made one pushcart that I used to deliver milk to several families for several years.

The gristmill was located in the center of town and managed by Mr. Craig Tyre. A large two-cycle gasoline engine pulled the mill; the end of the exhaust was placed in a 55-gallon metal drum under the floor of the gristmill. When the gristmill ran, the noise was heard all over town. Occasionally, Mr. Tyre let us help him pick the grooves in the heavy rocks which ground the corn into meal. He, like most of the men, drank "booze" occasionally. The other men made jokes about Mr. Tyre having too much booze one day and having the mill running so fast that he "unground" five pecks of meal back to corn before he could stop the mill. Mr. Tyre once stated that he had so many holes in his socks that he could put them on three different ways—from the top, the heel, or the toes.

The older men always played jokes or tricks on the young boys. One afternoon, my mother and I were walking to visit a neighbor. I was wearing short pants and no shoes. As we passed Dr. Moye's store, three of the older men were sitting in a Model T Ford car with metal running boards and no top. They invited me to come over to the car and look at some fish in a washtub in the backseat. When I stepped onto the metal running board, which had been connected to the car's magneto, I received one of the worst shocks I had ever received and was knocked off the running board.

The young boys also pulled jokes or tricks on each other. Gus had pulled a trick on me, and I looked forward to even the score. The opportunity presented itself the following Sunday afternoon. Gus was a favorite of one of his older relatives, who gave him a used Hudson automobile with red hubcaps and a canvas top with no side curtains. We were double dating that afternoon. He asked me to drive. My date and I were in the front seat, and he and his date were in the back seat. We were riding around in Brewton primarily, I think, to show off his Hudson automobile. He leaned over and whispered in my ear that he had to expel some gas. Realizing it was an ideal payback time, I whispered in his ear that I would blow the horn to signal him to expel the gas so that the horn would suppress his noise. I started blowing the horn, but I stopped about the time I thought he would expel the gas. The timing was perfect! When I stopped blowing the horn, he let the gas go. It was one of the loudest explosions I had ever heard. It sounded like the noise today when a plane breaks the sound barrier.

About 1935, James Maddox, who was five years older than the young men in our group, decided to build a hamburger and hot dog stand in Brewton. He got several slabs at a sawmill, old metal Coca-Cola signs, and some yellow paint that had been used by the highway department to paint the truss work timbers under highway bridges. After that building was completed, he painted the slabs with the yellow paint and named the business The Yellow Dog.

Frank Ballard was an older man whom everyone liked when he was sober. When he was intoxicated, Frank was mean. One Saturday night, a man who was a prizefighter traveling home to Wrightsville from Dublin stopped by the Yellow Dog to get a hot dog. Frank, drunk and unaware who the man was, entered and began to curse the prizefighter. The man invited Frank to go outside to settle their differences. The fighter beat Frank and threw him against the metal bars of Dr. Moye's store so hard that the bars bent. I obtained the bent bars and have kept them under a shelter for many years. The next morning, Frank's eyes were swollen shut, and his face looked like a piece of raw meat. After this incident, the name of the business was changed from *The Yellow Dog* to *The Bloody Bucket.* On another occasion, Frank was outside Dr. Moye's store when Mr. Sapp drove up in his car. Mr. Sapp was the father of Theron Sapp, the football player who broke the drought between UGA and Georgia Tech. When Frank threatened Mr. Sapp, he advised Frank that he had a pistol and would shoot him if he continued to threaten him and walk toward his car. Of course, Frank did not stop, so Mr. Sapp shot him twice in the abdomen. Although Frank fell, he got up and started walking home. Some of the men stopped him and carried him to the hospital in Dublin. After that, Frank always walked with a limp. Years later, he changed his life style, married a nice lady, and enjoyed a successful career.

In the springtime, we always had a "cleaning out," our parents' description of a horrible experience. They gave us a dose of Calomel at night. The next morning they gave us a dose of Epsom Salts to clean out the Calomel. They said the Calomel would "salivate" our stomachs if our stomachs were not cleaned out. I never got an explanation of what a salivated stomach meant. After we were "thoroughly" cleaned out, we had to take doses of 666 Tonic for thirty days. I never learned the benefits of taking the 666 Tonic.

Several times during the year, we cleaned the cow stables, hauled off the manure in a two-horse wagon, and spread the manure on the fields for fertilization. After the stables were cleaned, we hauled fresh pine straw and placed it in the stables. Because our wagon had high sides, we moved more straw in fewer loads. On one load, my brother and I had the straw piled high on the wagon. My brother was on top of the straw and threw his pitchfork to the ground. One of the tines on his pitchfork entered my left foot just below the ankle, came out the bottom of my foot, and stuck in the ground. We pulled the pitchfork out of the ground to release my foot.

Late that afternoon, while getting the cows to the lot, I waded through some stagnant water to get around the cows and head them toward the lot. About nine o'clock that night, my foot was swollen and infected. My father and a friend who was visiting us at the time carried me to Claxton's Hospital in Dublin. The nurses called Dr. Claxton, who came to the hospital to treat me. When Dr. Claxton and some nurses put me on an operating table, Dr. Claxton got something that appeared to be an oversized Q-Tip. He dipped the cotton in a bottle of Iodine and told my father and his friend to hold me. He rammed the swab through the wound and pulled the swab back out, gave me a tetanus shot, and told me my foot would be well in a few days. He was correct because I never had any problems with my foot after that incident.

My father and his brother were owners of Beall Brothers, a store selling general merchandise with current stock, large and complete. My father and his brother gave their customers calendars. I am fortunate to have a 1920 calendar. They even stocked caskets for display and sale in a back room in the store.

There was a man in town who enjoyed drinking alcohol. He had a habit of drinking too much, going into the store about closing time, and asking my father or uncle to keep the store open so that they could talk to him. They got tired of his habit. One night when he passed out, they put him into one of the caskets, closed the lid, and locked the store. The next morning when my father and his brother opened the store, they found their visitor gone and the panes and frame of a back window knocked out. They never had any trouble with him again. In 1926, they sold this store to another man; and shortly thereafter, he "sold the store to the Yankees."

In 1934, my father decided to open a grocery store of his own. He and some local carpenters constructed a forty-by-sixty-foot wood frame building. I was twelve years old and could hardly wait for the groceries and hardware to arrive. At that time sugar and rice came only in 100-pound bags and had to be weighed out, put in paper sacks, and wrapped with string according to how much a customer wanted. When the stock of goods arrived, the goods were dumped on the floor until my father, brother, and I could place them on the shelves. The candy, including the large Baby Ruth candy bars that were sold for five cents, was placed next to four sacks of sugar. I put a few groceries and other canned goods on the shelf, sat down on a sack of sugar, and ate one or two candy bars. My father, who was a strict disciplinarian, got tired of my procedure. He advised me to sit down and eat all the candy I wanted and then get back to work. I ate the top layer of candy bars and immediately became sick. After I had tossed my cookies a few times, my father instructed me to get back to work. I did, even though I was miserable.

The store building was a wood frame structure with wood floors, wood ceiling, and wood shingle roof. The two windows had iron bars; heavy oak two-by-four boards were wedged behind the doors to lock the building and to discourage robbery. The business volume increased annually. Most of the customers were farmers and had "run bills," which meant the store would carry the customers' credit account from January until they gathered and sold their crop in September or October. Most of the customers were honest and paid their accounts. However, there were always a few who did not pay their accounts. As a result, my father lost several hundred dollars every year.

Replica of Beall Grocery contructed in 1934.

When my father's store opened, there were two grocery stores in town. Each store had a hand-cranked telephone. There was a black man named Martin Lewis, a deacon in New Evergreen Church, who came to town on Saturday to get his groceries for the following week. He always asked everyone he met to give him a quarter for his church. Everyone liked Martin; consequently, he collected many quarters, which we hoped went to the church treasury. He always enjoyed teasing me and frequently talked about what a great man President Franklin Roosevelt was. One Saturday afternoon when Martin was in our store, I went over to the other store and used the telephone to call our store. I requested to speak to Martin Lewis. When he came to the phone, I informed him that I was President Franklin Roosevelt calling from the White House. Furthermore, I told him that I hoped he was turning in all the quarters he collected to the church treasury. In a flurry of excitement, he threw down the telephone receiver, ran out the front door of the store, and shouted, "Good God Almighty! The Pres-i-dent of the United States done called me!"

The roof over the gas tank on the front of the store had a light that stayed on all night and attracted all kinds of bugs. The bugs attracted frogs. Some nights we removed shots from a shotgun shell and rolled them in front of the frogs. The frogs grabbed the shots with their long tongue and swallowed them until they got too full and heavy to jump or even move.

When the business continued to grow, my father decided to build a new and larger store in 1968. The first store was Beall Grocery. The second store was Beall and Sons and remained in business until 1994. After my father and brother died, we closed the store.

There was a spring known as Rosa Spring on a farm we owned on U.S. Highway 80, which flowed about four hundred gallons of water per hour and had never run dry. The spring had been on the stagecoach route from Macon to Savannah and had provided a place where the passengers and horses could drink fresh water. In the '20s and '30s, the ladies in the area took their children there on Monday mornings to wash clothes in a log which the men had hewn out for that purpose.

My father always enjoyed inviting his friends to our place to cook fish and squirrel perlou and to grill steaks, so he decided to build a rustic cabin by the spring. He purchased a sawmill and cut the lumber off the farm, and I built most of the cabin. Some of my friends assisted with the plumbing and electrical work. The cabin has a large den, dining and kitchen area, one bedroom and a bathroom downstairs, and three bedrooms and one bathroom upstairs. A large sixteen-by-thirty-foot screened porch across the back of the cabin continues to be a pleasant setting for our fish fries and other meals in the spring and summer. The cabin has always provided an ideal place to entertain our family and friends. When my father entertained his friends, he referred to the cabin as "Husbands' Rest." However, when the cleaning of the cabin became my mother's responsibility, she referred to the cabin as "Buzzards' Roost."

Because the boys in my age group especially enjoyed quail hunting, we all had bird dogs. I owned bird dogs from the time I was seven years old. Two or three of us would get our dogs, guns and shells, a cinnamon roll, a can of pork and beans, and begin our hunting journey a little after daylight, hunt all day, and return home just before dark. We knew where the coveys were and killed many birds. Even then, we knew to leave a few birds in each covey so that they could raise more quail the following year. About 1975, when the quail began to disappear, my need for bird dogs decreased, and my interest in Boxer Bulldogs began. Consequently, I have owned many Bulldogs through the years.

I assume my brother and I were typical brothers. I thought I had to work harder than he did, and I am sure he felt the same way. This thought resulted in our having an occasional disagreement and even a few fights. On one occasion when one of the wage hands was sick, my father told my brother and me that I would plow in the morning and my brother would plow in the afternoon. My brother hid my basketball, which made me unhappy. I decided to even the score. There was a large persimmon tree that branched out over the road where he had to travel. I got a pocket full of green persimmons and climbed up the tree to a nice limb hanging over the road. Riding a skittish grey mule named "Queen," my brother calmly approached the persimmon tree. As soon as he rode under the tree, I unloaded a hand full of persimmons on the rump of the mule, and the mule threw him off. After he landed, I laughed.

Several older men were sitting on a loafers' bench across the road and saw what happened. They told my brother that the mule threw him so high in the air, that the bluebirds built a nest in his ears before he hit the ground.

He spotted me in the tree and realized what had happened. He started up the tree to get me, but I managed to get on the ground and started running down the W&T Railroad track to get away. However, he picked up a large, heavy, metal nut, threw it, and hit me in the back of the head. It knocked me out. Neither one of us got a whipping although both of us should have. I still have a knot on the back of my head where the nut hit.

Each year, cotton picking began about August and lasted until the crop was gathered. I always looked forward to that time so that I could pick cotton and earn enough money to buy a Barlow knife and my school clothes, which we ordered from Sears Roebuck. I used the knife primarily to peel sugar cane, which I enjoyed chewing. I have a deposit slip from the F&M Bank dated 1935 for fifty cents. The fifty cents was payment for two hundred pounds of cotton that I picked at twenty-five cents per hundred.

About 1925, the City Council hired Lewis Watson as City Marshal. He was a rather large man and enjoyed his whiskey. He did not enforce the drinking and drunk laws; and as a result, the ladies decided to run a slate of female candidates for the Mayor and City Council offices. The ladies won the election, and their first action was to fire the marshal. This might have been the beginning of the Women's Liberation Movement! After firing the marshal and handling the city business for a short time, the ladies returned that responsibility to the men. The older men indicated that the town was never the same after the ladies controlled the town for that short time.

Occasionally, the owner of a building would buy all the insurance he could obtain and then set the building on fire to collect the insurance money. This practice was normally referred to as "selling the building to the Yankees." I witnessed this one night as I was sitting on the side of my father's bed, which was located near a window where we could see uptown. A fire began in a wood framed grocery store owned by Ben Maddox, commonly known as Uncle Ben. The store was next to the F&M Bank, which was constructed of brick. On the other side of the bank building was a two-story wood framed dry goods store owned by I.E. Thigpen. When the fire from the Maddox store reached the Thigpen store, the bank building was completely engulfed in flames. My father and I assisted the cashier of the bank in moving some of the records from the bank before the fire got too hot.

Uncle Ben constructed another grocery store after "selling his original grocery store to the Yankees" and was known as one of the characters in town. His son, Claude, died at an early age and was buried in the first burial plot next to the front entrance gate to the Brewton cemetery. Someone asked Uncle Ben why he buried Claude so near to the front gate. He replied that when Gabriel blows his trumpet, he did not want all the other S.O.B.'s in the cemetery running over his son trying to get out of the gate.

Uncle Ben was the first customer in this area to purchase a Kelvinator refrigerator. It was such a large bulky contraption that it took five men to get it into his house. The power for running the refrigerator was furnished by burning kerosene. I never determined how a small flame from the kerosene caused the refrigerator to make ice and keep the storage area cool. Kelvinator did several advertising radio spots. The following was one of their best:

"Look at the beauty, Look at the price. Look at all the extra things that are nice. You can't go wrong with this advice, Get Nor, get Kelvinator."

When Uncle Ben and his wife died, the heirs sold their house to a young couple to whom I will refer as Mr. and Mrs. John Doe. The husband was a heavy drinker who would leave for two or three days on a drinking spree. On one occasion after being away for several days, he decided to send his wife a dozen red roses with a note saying he would be home the next day. When he returned, he saw all his clothes in twelve neat piles on the walk leading to the house. There was a red rose on top of each pile of clothes. You guessed it—he decided to wait another day to return home.

In 1934, the bank was robbed by a man named Elmo. He had robbed the ROTC Military Building at the University of Georgia and was taking the weapons to Cuba for sale in his private plane. Prior to robbing the bank, he had visited the White Swan, a beer joint in East Dublin located in the same vicinity as the East Dublin Post Office is today. He made the mistake of having too much to drink and showing the people his machine gun. On the morning that he robbed the bank, he cut the telephone wires from Brewton to Dublin. When he entered the bank, several men at the depot saw him enter with his machine gun. The depot agent notified the sheriff by telegraph. The sheriff had heard about Elmo's machine gun and learned that Elmo was staying at the Pritchett Place, just north of Dublin on Highway 441. They just waited until he arrived.

Although he had a good plan of escape, his delight in showing off the machine gun at the White Swan led to his arrest. After robbing the bank, he forced the cashier, Barton Herndon, to lie down on the running board of his stolen car. He slowed down about two miles from the bank and let Mr. Herndon get off. He drove the road to Blackshear's Ferry, abandoned the car, and crossed the Oconee River in a boat which he had placed there the day before the robbery. When he reached the other side of the river, he sank the boat and hid his loot in a large cypress stump with the intention of getting his car at the Pritchett farmhouse, returning to pick up the loot, and flying to Cuba in his plane. All the money except for a few coins was later recovered. The old timers said Mr. Keen, the bank president, cleaned up two acres of river swampland on his hands and knees, in an effort to find the coins that were not recovered. Elmo was sentenced to a few years in prison. After serving his time, Elmo returned to the F&M Bank in Dublin to see Mr. Herndon.

During this era, many people could not afford the use of a funeral home for a deceased family member. Therefore, someone in the community assisted the family in "laying out the dead." This procedure consisted of washing the body, dressing the body in a suit or dress, and placing the corpse in a coffin. The coffin was then placed in the living room of the family's home for viewing by the public. Normally, several people sat up at night at the home of the deceased.

When I was ten years old, Mr. Blankenship died, and I decided it was time for me to sit with the dead. I sat on the front porch with several of Mr. Blankenship's neighbors.

About 11:00 that night, everyone except one man had left. I decided to go into the living room to view the body. Just as I approached the coffin, I know I saw one of his arms move. I ran out of the house and slammed the porch screen door back against the wall. I jumped down the front steps and over a ditch about five feet wide and six feet deep between the road and the sidewalk and ran home so fast that the bottom of my feet felt hot.

When I arrived at my house, about three hundred yards from the Blankenship house, I jumped into the bed with my mother. After I related what had happened, she explained that it was just my imagination and encouraged me to go to sleep. After a short period of time, I did go to sleep; but that concluded my sitting up with the dead.

The older men were constantly teasing us about anything they thought appropriate. One of the worst occasions was when a boy's voice was changing. Dick Whitfield, who was about thirteen years old, rode a mule to Dr. Moye's store about noon one day to purchase five pounds of sugar and ten cents worth of ice. He carried a croaker sack so that he could place the ice in it. Dick rode the mule to the front door of the store, but he did not dismount. He yelled in a very high-pitched soprano voice that he wanted five pounds of sugar. Then in a low bass voice, he shouted that he wanted ten cents worth of ice. Mr. Tyre, the store clerk, was in the back of the store drawing some vinegar for another customer. He yelled back, "I will be there in a few minutes to help both of you!"

There were four churches in the town: two white churches and two black churches. All these churches cooperated in their community efforts. None of the churches had a preaching service every Sunday because the members could not afford to pay a full time preacher. The Baptist church had Sunday School every Sunday morning and Baptist Young People's Union every Sunday night. Church services were held once or twice a month. In 1948, the Baptists decided to become a full time church; thereafter, church services were held every Sunday.

The Baptist church was a wood framed structure about forty feet by sixty feet with a large room containing a pot-bellied stove and eight stove pipes, which heated the church in the winter time. The restroom was a two-holer outhouse located just to the rear of the church. Normally, the only thing in the outhouse was a Sears Roebuck catalogue. Occasionally, some of the mischievous boys in the church would place a bucket of red and white corncobs inside. It was "air conditioned" to the extent that one would freeze in the winter and burn up in the summer.

In the '40s, the ladies requested that the men install eyebolts in the walls and attach wire clotheslines, which reached across the width and length of the church. The ladies attached blue homespun cloth on metal rings and used these "curtains" to separate the church into Sunday School rooms.

One Sunday, after a particularly long-winded preacher had finally finished his sermon, the church held a conference to make a decision about painting the interior of the church. About 1:00 p.m., after a lengthy discussion by the ladies about the color to use, the moderator asked the men what they thought. Immediately, one man spoke up and informed the conference that as far as the men were concerned, they could use any color of paint for the interior of the church "from a honky-tonk red to a casket gray." After that remark, the members quickly decided to use white paint for the church interior.

Even though in the '20s and '30s we had church services once or twice a month, we always had a revival for one week in July, the hottest time of the year. The revival services were well attended, and there would be wagons and buggies parked all over the churchyard. The baptismal service at the conclusion of the week's services was usually held on Sunday afternoon at Brewton Creek or at a nearby pond. We had various types of preachers or evangelists—from those whose message was Hell, Fire, and Brimstone to those whose message was that God loved us so much that He would not send anyone to Hell.

In 1934, Mr. Edwards, a Mercer University student from Macon, led the revival. He and his wife stayed at our house for the week, and they brought their eleven-year old granddaughter with them. This young girl was probably one of the most effective evangelists I have ever heard. The Fox Theater in Atlanta had booked her to tap dance as their special attraction on Saturday nights. At that time, dancing was taboo among church people, so she informed the manager of the Fox that she was not going to dance anymore. Her words were that she "was not going to be the Devil's imp on Saturday night and God's angel on Sunday." When speaking at the revival, she stood in a pulpit chair so she could be seen. As a result of her message, we had eighteen additions to the church—twice as many as we had ever had. I joined the church that week and have been an active member since that time; I was an inactive member when I was a college student and a Marine during the war.

Original Brewton Baptist Church

I had the honor of serving as church treasurer, Sunday School superintendent, and the Intermediate boys' and girls' Sunday School teacher for twenty-five years. Realizing that Christian people need to express their viewpoints in a group, I requested that each student open the class with prayer and teach the Sunday School lesson once during the year. These students volunteered to offer the prayer and teach the lesson. During that time, only one student refused to participate. In later years, this student entered a political contest. After listening to one of his speeches, I was sure he realized he should have begun his public speaking sooner.

Brewton Baptist Church
Note the twelve white bricks on the front corners representing the twelve disciples.

After several years of discussing whether to add classrooms to the existing church or to build a new structure, the membership decided to erect a new church building. The Reverend J.M. Rainey, a physically crippled but spiritually strong pastor, and a small membership with great determination launched a building program. We planned to construct the educational building first, move into it, tear down the existing church building, and use its timbers for the new sanctuary. The timbers, mostly heart pine, were in excellent condition after sixty years. Work was begun on the sanctuary in January 1960 and was ready for occupancy in June 1960. Because various fundraising plans were implemented, the church was free of debt in 1966. A debt-free parsonage was dedicated in 1981, and a debt-free educational building was completed in 1983. Through the years, I was able to purchase the land surrounding the church to prevent any type of undesirable business from locating nearby.

My musical career was launched when I was ten years old. My mother, who was a music teacher for forty years and provided piano music for funerals, weddings, school programs, and church services, gave me piano lessons twice a week. I took lessons until I could play the song "The Big Bass Drummer." When some of my friends heard me play that song, they began to tease me about being a sissy and asked me if I wore lace on my underwear. That teasing concluded my piano career.

When I entered the ninth grade at Dublin High School, I joined the band, and my parents purchased a trumpet for me. There were six more trumpet players. Mr. Wiggins, the band director, asked for one of us to volunteer to play a baritone horn. I volunteered and enjoyed playing that horn the rest of the time I was in high school.

Having a very good director and a successful band, the Dublin High School band was invited to participate in various programs and parades. We entered state band competitions held in Milledgeville at Georgia State College for Women, and received very high ratings each year.

Curtis Beall is in the second row, fourth from left.

In 1940 when I was a senior, the director asked me to play a baritone solo in the state competition. I consented and played Leonard B. Smith's arrangement of "Ecstasy" at the Peabody Auditorium at Georgia State College for Women. Even though I was nervous and apprehensive, I received a superior rating. Since I was the only baritone solo participant, I always thought the judges were very liberal in their judging. After leaving high school, I put aside my music career to concentrate on athletics and college courses.

My friends and I were nineteen years old when the Japanese attacked Pearl Harbor. We knew it was a short time before we would be inducted into some branch of service. The ladies in the church purchased a silk flag. When a member of the church went into the service of our country, a gold star was sewn on the flag to represent that person. The stars were arranged to form a "V" for Victory. The flag was hung in the front of the church. Each time there was a meeting or special occasion, a prayer was offered for each serviceman.

Many of the men were involved in some of the worst battles of World War II. One in the Air Force was a bomber's navigator on a strike on the Polish oil fields. Thirty-four of the bombers were shot down. Another one in the Air Force was captured on Corrigador, was a Prisoner of War, and worked in the coal mines in Japan for four years. One was at Pearl Harbor when the Japanese attacked. He had just made the final payment on his new car, but the car was destroyed in the attack. Two of the men were in the Army in Burma with Merrill's Marauders. My brother was in the Marines with an amphibian tractor battalion in the invasion of Kwajalein, Guam, and Okinawa. I led an 81 MM mortar platoon of Marines in the battle for Okinawa and North China. Several men were in the invasion of Europe.

Of the seventeen members of our church who entered the service, every one returned after the war in reasonably good physical and mental condition. My mother saved the flag, which was framed and presented to the church along with a plaque listing the name of each serviceman represented in a special ceremony in 1994. As a constant reminder of the power of prayer, the flag and plaque are displayed appropriately in Brewton Baptist Church.

Dedicating World War II Victory Flag.

PLAYING BASKETBALL TO GET A COLLEGE EDUCATION

PLAYING BASKETBALL TO GET A COLLEGE EDUCATION

Chapter 2

The first time I remember handling a basketball was Christmas 1929. Santa brought my brother a basketball, two goals, and nets. He and I worked most of the day building two backboards, attaching the goals and nets, and cleaning up a small area for the basketball court. We sawed the poles for the backboards with a crosscut saw in the woods and carried the poles on our shoulders to the area where we would make our basketball court. Indoor courts and gymnasiums were nonexistent in rural areas at this time, so we drew the foul line and outside lines in the dirt. We, along with some of our friends, spent many hours practicing and playing on the dirt court. Prior to this, we used a fifty-five-gallon barrel hoop nailed on the side of a barn and a ball purchased at Woolworth's 5 & 10 Cent Store.

All the rural schools had similar dirt courts. Official games between schools were played on dirt courts until the late '30s, when the schools began to build wooden gymnasiums. One day when several of the boys at Brewton School were playing on the dirt court, a local character, George Thigpen, walked by the court with his rabbit dog and shotgun. One of the players threw the ball up in the air and told George to shoot the ball. With no hesitation, George raised his shotgun and shot the ball, which hit the ground with a plop. That concluded our ballgames until we could raise enough money to purchase another ball.

In the '30s, several of the smaller schools in the area voted to bond their district, consolidate with the Brewton School, and construct a new brick school building. The old wood frame Brewton School building was renovated and made into a basketball court. The interior walls were removed, the ceiling rafters were raised, overhead lights were installed, dishpans were used as reflectors for the lights, and the goals were installed.

There was only a small area left for spectators. Approximately one hundred people could be seated. The basketball court out-of-bound lines were eighteen inches from the outer walls on one side and at both ends, so players had to be careful not to hit the walls. Most of the windows were boarded up with sawmill slabs.

During one of the games, Hugh Maddox, a left-handed center for the Brewton team, drove to the basket for a crip shot. Just as Hugh jumped to shoot the ball, a big basketball player on the Mt. Carmel team gave him a shove on the shoulder, which caused Hugh to knock the slabs out the window and to land on the outside of the building. The game was stopped until he could walk around to the door on the other end of the building and re-enter the gym.

During rainy days and some days when we were not working, we chose teams composed of Brewton boys and played many competitive games. The size of each team depended on the number of available boys. The number varied from three to seven on each team. If there were not enough players to have a game, we practiced shooting set shots.

About 1938, several of the schools began to construct gymnasiums. Very little money was available from the local Board of Education, so each community financed and built its own gym. Fortunately, for the Brewton community, a local citizen and teacher, Gene Heckle, took the leadership. He and a group of other community leaders constructed a gymnasium. Several local landowners contributed pine trees, which were cut and hauled to the sawmill to be sawed into boards for the construction of the gym. Local volunteers handled this part of the project. The ladies were busy raising money to pay for the electrical equipment, metal roof, and pot-bellied wood burning stoves for heat. These ladies sponsored several events to raise money: cake walks, homemade cake raffles, and various types of suppers. When all the money and material for the construction had been accumulated, volunteers completed the construction in about one year. The gym had a dressing room for the local and visiting team, but there were no showers or restrooms. When the old gym was torn down, the salvaged material was used in the new gym. The new gym was utilized extensively for school and community affairs.

In 1937, I was attending school in Dublin and decided to participate in the basketball team tryouts.

I made the team and was elected captain by my teammates in 1937, 1938, and 1939. Arlington Kelly, a Duke graduate and athlete, was the coach.

Years later, Coach Kelly became a World War II B-29 pilot. After the war when he and his crew were flying home, they stopped in Kwajalein for fuel. When they took off, the plane fell into the ocean. The entire crew died in the tragic accident.

Curtis Beall,
Dublin High School, 1938

The Dublin gym on North Calhoun Street was known as the Hargrove Gym. The gym was a wooden structure with adequate seating for spectators and dressing rooms with showers. However, the players had to build a fire in a wood burning stove to heat the water. We decided that using this method to take showers at the gym was too much trouble; therefore, we waited until we returned home to bathe after practice and games.

I rode to high school in Dublin every morning with two men who were employees of the Farmers and Merchants Bank, which had moved from Brewton to Dublin. Frequently, however, I had to find another ride home after practice and games. Occasionally, I caught the W & T (Wrightsville & Tennille) train to Brewton if practice was over in time. The fare to ride the W & T was 15 cents. If I missed the train and could not get another ride, I walked a distance of seven miles to my home. I tried to avoid walking after a hard practice or game. Because I desired a basketball scholarship to college, I was willing to make the sacrifice.

Dublin High School sweater
Dublin, Georgia

The players on this Dublin team were Moody Brown, Charlie Waller, Roy Bedingfield, Sonny Clark, Olin Kersey, Joe Stanley, Frarrie Smalley, Edward Sheppard, and I. In 1937, we had a good record. In 1938 and 1939, we played in the final game for the district championship. In 1938, the District Tournament was played in Montezuma; the championship game was played between Eatonton and Dublin. Eatonton had the three Griffis brothers, who had played basketball together since they were children, and two other tall men who played with them. Our coach, as well as all the Dublin players, knew we did not have a chance to win against Eatonton. Our coach told us to "freeze the ball" on every play and to slow the game down every way possible. We carried out his instructions, but the spectators began to "boo" us every time we got the ball. Even with those instructions, we still lost the game by several points. The Eatonton team won the State Basketball Championship, defeating its opponent by thirty points. Moreover, Eatonton's basketball team was truly superior.

I was selected as an All District Player in 1938 and 1939. I received basketball scholarship offers from several colleges as a result of the All District Player recognition. I accepted a scholarship to Middle Georgia College in Cochran, Georgia. The college was only forty-five miles from my home, Jake Morris was a very successful coach, and several of the team members were outstanding players. I anticipated a successful basketball season. We had an excellent record and won the State Junior College Championship in Tifton, Georgia, in 1940, the year of the new gym dedication at Abraham Baldwin Agricultural College. Several of the players on this team became outstanding high school coaches in later years.

Curtis Beall at Middle Georgia College, 1941

After one year at Middle Georgia, I transferred to UGA. Under NCAA rules, a one-year transfer student was ineligible to play on a senior college varsity basketball team. I practiced with the UGA team, but I was not allowed to play in an official game. Coach Lampp encouraged me to continue my basketball career. The UGA team was not very successful, and I am sure that I could have made the team if I had been eligible.

I was ordered to active duty in the USMC on July 1, 1943, to be stationed at Duke University. There were approximately 160 students from UGA in this group, including several members of the 1942 UGA Rose Bowl football team. When some of the other Marine students informed the Duke University coach that I had played basketball in junior college, he invited me to try out for the Duke team. I joined the team and enjoyed playing with a group of outstanding basketball players who had played at Mississippi State, University of Mississippi, Virginia, Maryland, and other colleges. We won most of our games and the Southern Conference, which is presently the ACC. The Duke coaches were firm believers that every player must be in excellent physical condition. One of the most difficult exercises required us to run up and down on the bleachers in Cameron Football Stadium. Apparently, based on our winning record, the coaches' thinking was correct.

I never lost sight of the fact that I was playing basketball to get a college education and degree.

Middle Georgia College sweater
Cochran, Georgia

Middle Georgia Basketball Team, 1941
Curtis Beall is second from left in the second row.

Gymnasium and Indoor Stadium, Duke University, Durham, North Carolina

Duke University jacket
Durham, North Carolina

THE GIRL OF MY DREAMS

THE GIRL OF MY DREAMS

Chapter 3

Like most young men, I had a few girlfriends. As I grew older, and after being raised in a conservative, disciplined, religious home, I had very definite ideas about the qualities I wanted in a girlfriend and a wife.

One day while riding a bus in Athens, Georgia, on the University of Georgia campus going east on Broad Street, I saw a girl walking across the street from the Varsity, directly across from the Arch on the corner of Broad and College Street. She was the most beautiful girl I had ever seen. She was wearing saddle oxfords, a purple skirt, and a purple sweater. In fact, I got off the bus when it stopped at the Arch and tried to locate her, but I was unsuccessful.

About two weeks later, I attended a dance at Pound Auditorium on Coordinate Campus, and the first person I saw was the girl I had seen crossing the street. She was wearing a purple evening dress and was even more beautiful than when I saw her the first time. I interrupted her dance with another boy and learned she was June Clarke and lived in Athens. I finally persuaded her to give me her phone number.

We had a date the following weekend and had occasional dates until Little Commencement, when I invited her to be in the Lead Out with me. The non-fraternity men had the Lead Out at Little Commencement and the fraternity men at Homecoming. As Campus Leader, June and I led the Lead Out. The band played "Stardust." We had agreed to be friends prior to this event. However, the more I learned about her, the more I appreciated her. My mother, with whom I had a close relationship, gave me good advice. She always told me that "beauty is only skin deep" and that what is on the inside is more important than what is on the outside. Because June possessed all the qualities I wanted in a girlfriend and a wife, I knew she was the person I wanted in my life forever.

Curtis Beall and June Clark in the Lead Out.

June Clarke, 1942

Since I could not afford a car, most of our dates were walking dates. Fortunately, we both enjoyed walking. On weekends, we walked over Ag Hill, by the Dairy Barn, and over the Horticultural Farm, which is now where the Intramural athletic fields are located.

Georgia Power had erected two cables across the Oconee River. To cross the river, a person walked on one cable and held onto the other cable, which was about chest high. I never heard of any student who fell into the river. June and I walked on the cable and issued each other dares to fall into the river. Present day slang would call that "playing chicken." That probably was a more apt description since I was the rooster and she was the hen.

As Campus Leader, I was given free tickets to the movies, so we saw most of the good movies. We also enjoyed "courting" in the Victory Garden, located just off Lumpkin Street. We were getting to be more than just friends when I received orders from the USMC to report to Duke University on July 1, 1943, for active duty. Attempting to get my degree prior to entering the service, I had attended UGA continuously since entering in 1941. I had completed all the required courses except bacteriology, which I completed when I returned to UGA in 1947, after I had served in the Marine Corps in World War II for three and one-half years.

We wrote each other occasionally. She was completing her education at UGA and dating other boys, and I was dating other girls while I attended Duke. However, dating other girls was not as enjoyable as dating June.

The Marine Corps granted us a one-week leave in December 1943. Intending to see June, I decided to return to my home in Brewton. Circumstances were not favorable because transportation at the time was difficult to arrange. I thumbed a ride to Raleigh, North Carolina, and intended to purchase a ticket on The Silver Meter train to Savannah. The waiting line to purchase tickets was about three blocks long, and the ticket agent indicated no seats would be available unless someone cancelled a reservation. I decided that if I was to get home for Christmas, I must make other arrangements. I hitched a ride to the Raleigh-Durham Airport. When I arrived at the airport terminal, I saw a B-26 bomber land and two pilots exiting the plane. As they walked to the terminal, I met them and asked their destination. They were delivering a new plane to Hunter Air Force Base in Savannah, and they offered me a ride. Since there were no seats in the plane, I sat on a parachute until we arrived safely in Savannah. I walked a short distance to U. S. Highway 80 and thumbed a ride to Dublin and then to my home in Brewton. GA. After enjoying four days at home, I traveled to Duke by the same method as I had traveled to Brewton and arrived back on time.

I received my military training at various bases on the East Coast, (See short story on Tour of Duty in the Marine Corps), and was ordered to report to Camp Pendleton, California, by January 1, 1945.

June was completing her Home Economics degree at UGA. While at the university, she was elected Ag. Hill Beauty Queen, and the Cooperative Extension Service printed her picture on the front of several of their brochures. After she graduated from college, she began teaching kindergarten and lived in Atlanta.

I assume that the old saying "absence makes the heart grow fonder" related to June and me because we began to correspond more frequently. I was given a ten-day leave, including travel time, prior to reporting to Camp Pendleton. I stayed at home for five days and planned to have two days with June. Fortunately, I had three days with her. I was scheduled to travel to the West Coast on Eastern Airlines under orders. Due to weather conditions, the planes could not land or take off for twenty-four hours at Atlanta's Hartsfield Airport. It was customary at the time for the airline to pay the hotel bill if there was a flight delay, so I had an extra day at the Henry Grady Hotel at no expense—and to see June. The night before I was scheduled to leave early the next morning, June and I went to Grant Park, which was safe at that time. Because it was a very cold night, June's topcoat was not warm. We decided that both of us should wrap up in my officer's overcoat. I have not determined yet how we both wrapped ourselves in my overcoat. I gave her a gold bracelet with her name on one side and my name on the other side. I told her I was placing the bracelet on her arm until I could put a ring on her finger. We assumed that night that we were engaged to be married if and when I returned home after World War II.

I boarded a plane at seven the next morning and flew to Dallas-Fort Worth Airport, from there to Los Angeles, and reported to Camp Pendleton for duty at 8:00 a.m., January 1, 1945. I was in training there for about three months and boarded the *Admiral Hughes*, a converted cruise liner with six thousand other Marines for duty overseas. (See story on Tour of Duty in USMC for details.) June and I wrote letters to each other daily, except during the time I was in combat. Her letters were always a great morale booster for me. We also read Psalm 91, which was comforting, every day when possible.

After combat and overseas duty for twelve months, I was ordered back to the States. After eighteen days aboard ship, four hundred other Marines and I arrived in San Francisco. What a sight! How happy I was to travel under the Golden Gate Bridge, depart from the ship, and return to the States. I stayed overnight in the St. Francis Hotel in San Francisco, which was the first time in a year that I had slept in a bed. I flew to Los Angeles the next day and then to Dallas-Fort Worth on Eastern Airlines. At that time, planes carried approximately thirty passengers. We were in an electrical storm over the Grand Canyon. The plane was somewhat like a cork on water on a windy day. However, I never saw such beautiful colors as when the lightning flashed and reflected off the various types of rocks in the canyon. We made it safely to Dallas-Fort Worth and to Atlanta.

I arrived at 3:00 a.m. June and two of her roommates met me at the airport, and we took a taxi to their boarding house at 1447 Peachtree Street. During the ride to her boarding house, I had the longest kiss I ever had. The only time we were not kissing during the ride was when we had to get air. What a kiss! Without being asphyxiated, we arrived safely at the boarding house, where June and her five friends had two bedrooms and one bathroom. June and her roommates moved into one bedroom so that I could use the other bedroom. After sleeping a few hours after a very short night, I needed a shower and entered the bathroom after they left for work. All of them had been friends at UGA, had earned their degrees there, and were now kindergarten teachers. I entered the bathroom to find more lingerie hanging on the shower rod, on wall hangers, and on fixtures than I had ever seen! After surviving combat, making the trip safely over the Grand Canyon, and being overseas, I decided that the safest thing to do was to take a "spit bath" and not take a chance on hanging myself on bra straps and other ladies' under garments.

I enjoyed spending time with June another day and then boarded a bus for Dublin. My parents did not have a home phone, so I called a family friend and president of the Farmers and Merchants Bank in Dublin, Mr. Lehman Keen. He met me at the bus station and carried me home. Words cannot adequately express how happy I was to be at home again with my family.

After a couple of weeks, I returned to Atlanta to spend time with June for a couple of days so that we could discuss plans for our wedding and the completion of my education. We purchased her engagement and wedding rings at Atlanta's Bennett's Jewelry Store. During this trip, I gave her the engagement ring.

We set the date, May 18, 1946, for our wedding at the First Baptist Church in Athens, where June was a member. The Reverend Jim Wilkinson, pastor of the church, performed the marriage ceremony. The reception was in the YWCA, which was directly across the street from the church.

June Clarke becomes the bride of Curtis Beall, May 18, 1946, in First Baptist Church, Athens.

Because it was impossible to purchase a vehicle at this time, my brother let us use his car to go on our honeymoon. After the reception, we drove to Atlanta to spend our first night at the Henry Grady Hotel. In attempting to get in the hotel parking lot, we got on a one-way street going in the wrong direction. Fortunately, a nice motorcycle cop stopped us and volunteered to lead me around the block so that I could enter the parking lot. He saw the "Just Married" sign on our car and advised me that I was about to get on many one-way streets going in the wrong direction! I do not think June particularly liked his joke.

We had a good night's sleep the first night and left for a week's stay at the Greystone Hotel in Gatlinburg, Tennessee. At the time, money was worth considerably more than it is today. We purchased a full country breakfast for $.35, lunch for $1.10, and dinner for $2.25. At the end of the week, we went to my parents' home for a week before I resumed my education at UGA. Since housing for married couples was difficult to find, June's parents invited us to stay with them until I received my Bachelor of Science degree with a major in Agronomy and a minor in Animal Husbandry. On completion of my education at UGA, we moved in with my parents. I began farming and teaching a veterans' agriculture class at Dexter High School and later at Rentz High School. I received my diploma by mail later.

Our first child, Anita, was born May 26, 1948. We decided to build our first house. I had some leave time accumulated, so I took off thirty days to construct the house. I employed four carpenters, their helpers, and one brick mason. We completed the house and moved in within the thirty-day period. Our second child, Al, was born on January 18, 1953.

We really enjoyed living in our first house until 1979, when we built our second house on a 465-acre farm I had purchased on U.S. Highway 80, eight miles east of Dublin. We really enjoy living in this location and hope to live here until the Grim Reaper calls us home.

June became a Christian in 1936 and joined the First Baptist Church in Athens. Since that time, she has been very active in her Christian life. She joined the Brewton Baptist Church in 1947 and has served as Sword Drill Director, Baptist Training Union teacher, Sunday School teacher, Women's Missionary Union President, Vacation Bible School Principal, and Family Night Hostess for many years. Some of the young people who are leaders in our community and church today comment on the good influence she has been on their lives.

Unfortunately, she had a minor stroke on July 21, 2000, and a major stroke on November 3, 2000. After she suffered from her first stroke, we took her to Mayo Clinic in Jacksonville, Florida, for a series of tests. The Mayo Clinic doctors did not find the cause of her problem. According to our local doctors, the second stroke was caused by atrial fibrillation of the heart, which caused the release of blood clots and brain damage. Since the last stroke, she has made considerable progress from the wheelchair, to the walker, and to a walking stick. Today, with assistance, she walks approximately one mile outside and exercises inside daily. She enjoys returning to Athens and especially looks forward to returning for all the home football games. We stay in a handicapped room at the Continuing Education Center. A member of our family and June watch the game on television while other family members attend the game.

We both know that if people nourish the spiritual phase of their lives, the other phases of life will assume their proper places. We have enjoyed life together for sixty years, and our love for each other grows stronger every year. She is still the "Girl of My Dreams," even more so now. My prayer is that I can live to take care of her as long as she lives.

The Bealls celebrate their sixtieth anniversary.

THE NATION AND UGA, THE YEAR GEORGIA WON THE ROSE BOWL

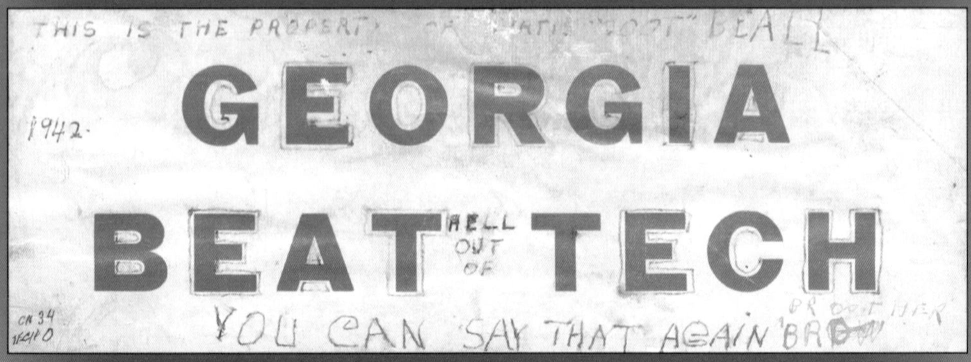

THIS IS THE
1942
GEORGIA
BEAT
HELL
OUT
OF
TECH
YOU CAN SAY THAT AGAIN

THE NATION AND UGA, THE YEAR GEORGIA WON THE ROSE BOWL

Chapter 4

The conditions in the nation and on the UGA campus were considerably different in the late '30s and early '40s, an era prior to MRIs, CAT scans, radar and sonar, cortisone, food freezers, contact lens, and birth control pills. During this time, we thought abstinence was a better way to control pregnancy. It was also prior to cell phones, credit cards, computers, electric typewriters, dishwashers, panty hose, air conditioners, ATMs, and before man's dream of landing on the moon.

I assume many young people today think our generation was very odd. We married first and then lived together. A closet to us was a place where we hung our clothes, not for "coming out of." Having a meaningful relationship meant getting along well with our friends and relatives. This was prior to gay marriages, house husbands, lady CEOs, marriages by computer and the Internet, artificial insemination, artificial hearts, and transplanted organs. None of the male students would have worn earrings. If any had been brave and worn earrings, they probably would have lost the rings and part of their ears. The National Anthem was sung as it was written. A grocery store meant a place to buy groceries, time meant actual time, and a person's word was his bond. Most clothing, appliances, automobiles, and machinery were produced in the United States of America and were stamped accordingly. The term "making out" described a person's outcome after some type of mental or physical examination.

Students rally to express approval when Georgia beats Ole Miss.

There were Five and Ten Cent Stores, where items could be purchased for five and ten cents. For five cents, a person could make a phone call if a pay phone could be located. A customer could buy a soft drink, a stamp, or purchase five one-cent postcards. A car could be purchased for $700, and gas could be purchased for eleven cents per gallon. The problem was that only a few people could afford the car or the gas. Cigarette and cigar smoking were fashionable and encouraged because smoking was prevalent in movies and in printed media.

Grass was a plant for lawns and pastures, dope was a soft drink such as Coca Cola, pot was a cooking utensil, and aides were people who assisted others in various tasks. We knew the difference between the sexes, but we knew nothing about a sex change. We used what the Good Lord had given us. I assume we were naïve to believe a woman needed a husband to have a baby.

Entering the University of Georgia was not a problem if a student had average grades and paid the required fees. Registration was available in the Holmes Academic Building, located next to the Arch. When a freshman entered the university, one of the first items he/she acquired was a Rat Cap. Freshmen wore these at all times except when they were inside buildings. Rat Court was conducted every Monday night in the lobby of the dormitory. The freshmen were questioned about their grades. If they were having problems with their grades, these students were encouraged by various methods to improve. If necessary, some of the upper classmen volunteered to assist them.

An annual treat for freshmen was the Shirt-Tail Parade.

Freshmen were not allowed to walk under the Arch until the first quarter was completed and the boys had participated in the Shirt Tail Parade. All the students anticipated this event every year. The boys removed their pants and wore only their shirts and shorts. The upper classmen formed a double line and gently struck the freshmen's rear ends with a belt as the freshmen ran between the two lines. The freshmen began their trek at the Arch and ended at Coordinate Campus.

Most of the male students resided in Candler Hall, Old College, Joe Brown, Clark Howell, and Camp Wilkins. A few male students resided in boarding houses or private homes located primarily along Lumpkin Street. Those who joined fraternities lived in the fraternity houses, which were located mainly along Lumpkin Street and Milledge Avenue.

The freshman female students lived in dormitories on Coordinate Campus, which was approximately one and one-half miles from Main Campus. Except for those who joined sororities and lived in the sorority houses located mainly on Milledge Avenue, the other female students lived in dormitories on South Campus.

My brother, M.F. Beall, Jr., preceded me as a student at the University of Georgia. He was a freshman in 1936 and lived in Candler Hall. I visited him a few times and chose to live in Candler Hall as well. After attending Middle Georgia College in Cochran, Georgia, as a freshman, I entered UGA in 1941 as a sophomore. (See short story on basketball career.) Candler Hall, compared to today's standards, was not a very convenient dormitory. In the first room on the right from the front door was proctor Wilson Hudson's room. On the left was the large lobby, which was furnished with five or six broken chairs and a rough wooden table approximately six feet by ten feet with one broken leg. The banisters on the stairs were broken most of the time. The boys who lived in a fraternity house across the street had broken many of the windows on the Lumpkin Street side of the dorm with pellet rifles and slingshots, and many of their windows facing Lumpkin Street were also broken. The showers, usually with cold water only, were located in the basement. Radiators connected to a coal furnace in the basement heated the dormitory. However, these inconveniences were offset by the pleasure of knowing and living with a group of good students.

Dean Wills, a black custodian, informed us that he got his several diplomas together with Uncle Tom Reed, who got his black derby and walking stick, and they were the ones who came to Athens and really started the university. Dean Wills had one vice: He loved moonshine whiskey.

Living in Candler Hall were twin boys from the North Georgia Mountains. Apparently, they had a good source of moonshine whiskey. We realized that when they returned from visiting their parents, Dean Wills got drunk and passed out on the basement coal pile. Therefore, we had only cold water for showers and shaves.

Although the room doors were not locked, I was aware of only one incident of stealing. A freshman student from New Jersey lived in a room on the front of the dormitory on the third floor. Some of the men in that section began to miss several items such as wristwatches and money. This student had been observed going into some of the rooms when the occupants were not present. One morning when the suspect was in class, some of the upper classmen decided to search his room. When they found several stolen items, they threw all his clothes, bed linens, and all his personal items out the window. When the student returned from class, he saw what had happened. We assumed he left the university because we never saw or heard anymore from him.

Watching late movies was popular on Wednesday nights. Some of the students filled balloons with water and went up on the roof of the dormitory, which looked almost directly down on the sidewalk on Lumpkin Street. These students threw the water balloons close to the pedestrians who were on the sidewalk returning from the movie. Pedestrians decided to cross over to the other side of the street before they passed Candler Hall.

I roomed on the top floor in the northwest corner of the dormitory with Britt Bacon and Dean Duggan from Irwinton, Georgia. We purchased a radio from an Athens junk shop; unfortunately, it could only broadcast one station. It began playing at seven o'clock every morning and served as our alarm clock. A "Hell Fire and Brimstone" preacher started the day. He said he was going to preach "Heaven High, Hell Deep, and Gun Barrel straight"!

Britt was a member of a family of eight boys and two girls. His mother was a schoolteacher and apparently did an excellent job in teaching her children the English language. Frequently, at night when we retired, Dean and I pronounced a word that we found in the dictionary. Britt spelled, pronounced, defined, and used the word correctly for us. Then we followed his pattern to learn the word. Britt and Dean were business majors and had successful careers. Britt was Comptroller with Trust Company of Georgia, and for many years, he read aloud all business bills presented to the Georgia House of Representatives. Britt died in 2001. Dean was Comptroller for the Life of Georgia Insurance Company until he retired. Approximately thirty days after retirement, Dean was painting the eaves on his two-story house and tragically fell off the ladder and was killed.

There was a friendly competition between the boys in Candler Hall and Old College. The week before Thanksgiving, the Athletic Department let us borrow the Georgia football uniforms to compete with each other in Sanford Stadium. The spectators were offered moonshine whiskey furnished by the boys from the mountains and served from a washtub. The cost for a person to enter the stadium to view the game was the contribution of some type of canned food, which was distributed later to needy families at Thanksgiving. This game became known as The Whiskey Bowl.

Most of us grew up in rural areas or in small towns and would occasionally seine Lake Karoda and get out in the woods to have a fish fry. The area where Lake Karoda was located is now the location of the Veterinary School. Most of the courting occurred on River Road or in some secluded area on campus. Some students favored Sanford Stadium and the baseball field as courting areas.

Practically all the dances were held in Woodruff Hall on Main Campus or Pound Auditorium on Coordinate Campus. We had several big name bands to perform for the dances: Tommy Dorsey, Jimmy Dorsey, Sammy K., and Glenn Miller. Popular songs of the time that were played at these dances included "Stardust," " I'll Never Smile Again," "Don't Sit Under The Apple Tree," " Deep In The Heart Of Texas," " The White Cliffs of Dover," " Chattanooga Choo-Choo," "Tennessee Waltz," " Don't Fence Me In," " God Bless America" by Kate Smith, "Deep Purple," " You Made Me Love You," and "Moonlight Serenade."

Many of the boys living in dormitories majored in agriculture and walked to Ag Hill for classes. There was a dirt clay walk from Sanford Stadium up to Conner Hall, so in wet weather we either slipped and slid on the dirt walk, or we walked up Lumpkin Street and then back to Conner Hall on Cedar Street. Because there were very few students who owned cars, parking was not a problem.

UGA began a male cheerleading program in the '30s. The female cheerleading program began in 1940. The students elected the cheerleaders. One cheerleader was elected by the fraternity boys, one by the sorority girls, one by the non-fraternity campus boys, and one by the non-sorority campus girls. I was elected cheerleader by the campus boys in 1941 to cheer in 1942 and 1943. Britt Bacon, one of my roommates, was one of my campaign managers. He went home one weekend and printed the campaign cards on the newspaper printing press in Irwinton, Georgia. We ran our campaign on a "shoe string" budget, but it proved to be quite successful. Later in 1941, I was also elected and served as Campus Leader.

The State of Georgia had men of excellent leadership in Congress who understood the world situation and helped to prepare the nation prior to the declaration of war by Franklin Roosevelt in December 1941. In the late '30s, Representative Carl Vinson from Milledgeville was Chairman of the House Naval Affairs Committee and succeeded in getting House approval to fund and build a stronger navy. Senator Richard Russell from Winder was Chairman of the Senate Armed Services Committee and was successful in getting the funding to expand the other services.

Cherleaders Kathryn Rice and "Coot" Beall chase a couple of gobblers down on the ranch, November 1942

Everyone who was knowledgeable about current events knew America was preparing to enter World War II. The Germans were posting their submarines in the Atlantic Ocean off the U.S. east coast and sinking hundreds of cargo ships carrying weapons and other material to England. This threat was eventually overcome when the ships were placed in convoys and protected by warships and aircraft. After President Roosevelt declared war on Japan following the attack on Pearl Harbor on December 7, 1941, the nation was on a wartime footing. Food, gas, and other items were rationed, and the mood of the people and students was to do everything possible for the war effort.

A temporary platform to be used for a student rally to encourage students to do more for the war effort was constructed on the sidewalk just back of the UGA Chapel Building. As Campus Leader, I was asked to speak.

Any boys or men between the ages of eighteen and forty who were physically fit were required to register for the draft. The UGA student enrollment decreased because so many boys were going into the Armed Forces. The administration sent out a three-man team: Bobby Lipchutes, President of the Interfraternity Council and later legal advisor to President Jimmy Carter; a professor, and me as Campus Leader to visit high schools to encourage students to attend UGA. We visited schools in Macon, Albany, Cordele, LaGrange, and Columbus. After completing our visit in Columbus, we could not find an available room. The professor drove out to Phenix City, Alabama, where we found a room. At the time, Phenix City had the reputation of having more "Houses of Ill Repute" than any other city of similar size in the country. The professor locked Bobby and me in our room, and he left. We never learned where he went, but we seriously doubted if his destination was related to school business.

Prior to this time, most of the American work force was composed of men. Because many men were volunteering or being drafted into the various services, the women began to perform jobs previously held by men. One of the popular cartoons of the day was a picture of a woman in work clothes, hard hat, tools in her hand, entitled "Rosie the Riveter." Another famous cartoon posted throughout the country was a picture of a man with his finger across his lips indicating silence and captioned "A slip of the lip may sink a ship."

Most of the services had programs in which a college student could stay in college until he was ordered to active duty. I joined the U.S. Marine Corps in September 1942 and remained in college until I was ordered to active duty at Duke University on July 1, 1943. During this same period, I was elected to X-Club, Aghon, Blue Key, Gridiron, and ODK. I served as President of Blue Key, Secretary-Treasurer of Gridiron, and was voted by the student body as Outstanding Senior in a campus-wide election and awarded a loving cup pictured here.

Red and Black

's Pre-Eminent College Weekly—Celebrating Our 50th Anniversary

IVERSITY OF GEORGIA, ATHENS, GEORGIA, APRIL 9, 1943. No. 24—Z-

Arnaldo Estrella, Noted Pianist, Closes Concert Series Monday; Beall Named Outstanding Senior

To Receive 'X' Club Cup

Gus Partee Second, Jim Perry Third

Curtis "Coot" Beall, Brewton, was elected outstanding senior of the year in the campus wide election held Wednesday. He will be awarded the silver cup given by the "X" Club within the near future.

Of the 418 votes cast, Beall received over 200 of them. Gus Partee was second in the voting and Jim Perry third. The other candidates were Willis Johnson, fourth, and Robert Lipshutz, fifth.

Clifford Martin, president of the "X" Club, said that he was well satisfied with the number of votes cast and stated that he felt that the students had cooperated very nicely in the election. Booths for the voting were placed on all three of the campuses, and the voting was evenly distributed.

Beall, a transfer student from Middle Georgia Junior College, has shown great interest in the activities here on the campus. He was a cheer leader during his junior year and was elected campus leader in the fall quarter election. Besides these honors he is a member of many honorary clubs on the campus. He is president of Blue Key, president of Gridiron, secretary-treasurer of "X" Club, member of Aghon rnd ODK.

Curtis Beall wears the X-Club jacket signifying his selection as Outstanding Senior at UGA in 1943.

The Navy decided to use the dormitories and many of the classrooms in 1942; consequently, students were forced to find another place to live. A bachelor lawyer who lived and practiced law in Athens had acquired extensive Athens real estate. He invited twenty students, mostly from Candler Hall, to live in a large two-story house that he owned on Hill Street. He agreed to be our housemother, added a couple of showers, and placed beds in the rooms. We moved from our dormitory to our new quarters, which we named Buckingham Palace. This lawyer was C.O. (Fat) Baker, who weighed approximately four hundred pounds. He was a member of most of the campus organizations and enjoyed participating in them for many years, especially Demosthenian. After the war, he was elected Representative from Clarke County and was the largest person ever to be elected to the House of Representatives. An especially large chair was made for him when he was elected.

Loving Cup presented to Outstanding Senior, Curtis Beall.

He always wanted to be Governor of Georgia and began his campaign in the late '40s. When he came to Dublin to make a campaign

Buckingham Palace residents. Curtis Beall is second from left, top row.

speech, I invited him to visit with our family and to spend the night. As a precaution, I put two or three extra slats under the bed. Apparently, three slats were not sufficient. About 2:00 a.m. I heard a loud noise and felt the house shake. I rushed to his room and saw that he was not hurt, but he was still on the mattress, which was on the floor. He slept that way the rest of the night.

The Axis during WWII was Germany, Italy, and Japan. The Allies were the United States, Great Britain, China, France, Australia, New Zealand, and other smaller countries. The war did not go well for the Allies in the beginning. The Germans conquered Poland, Rumania, Czechoslovakia, Belgium, The Netherlands, and France in a short period of time. During this same time, the Japanese conquered Manchuria, The Philippines, Dutch East Indies, Singapore, Guam, Wake, and other Pacific Islands.

The mood of the people in America was grim. Realizing the people needed a morale booster, President Roosevelt summoned the Army Chief of Staff, General George Marshall; the Chief of Staff of the Army, Air Force General "Hap" Arnold; and the Chief of Naval Operations, Admiral Ernest King, and advised them to devise a plan to attack Japan. They advised the president that such a plan would be impossible. However, the president was persistent in fulfilling his command. After several weeks, these leaders devised a plan to launch twin-engine B-25 Mitchell land-based bombers from an aircraft carrier deck. The plane had a sixty-seven-foot wingspan and weighed fourteen tons.

Jimmy Doolittle was selected to train the men who would be involved and to lead the raid on Japan. A group of 140 pilots and their crews who were training in Oregon volunteered for the mission. After several weeks of training, these men were ready to execute the plan, which seemed very simple, but was very difficult to execute.

The aircraft carrier *Hornet* with the land-based bombers aboard would approach an area within five hundred miles of Japan to launch the sixteen bombers. The Japanese assumed that they were safe from air attacks because land-based aircraft could not reach their homeland from Midway or Hawaii and that any aircraft carriers would be destroyed if they sailed too close to Japan. The plan was that the planes would be launched in the afternoon, and the carrier and supporting vessels would head back to Pearl Harbor under cover of darkness. The bomber crews would drop their bombs over the cities at sunset, fly to an airfield in Chucho China, and be guided to the airfield by homing beacons.

As so often happens in that area, the weather took a turn for the worse. Because the wind was so strong and the waves were so high, it was necessary for the Navy deckhands and the plane crews to crawl on all fours across the deck to keep from washing overboard.

Prior to reaching the planned launch point, two Japanese picket boats observed the American ships and radioed a warning to Tokyo. Destroyers sank the picket boats although the damage had already been done.

The *Hornet's* captain informed Jimmy Doolittle they had lost the element of surprise and that it would be best to launch the bombers even though they were approximately eight sailing hours and two hundred miles short of the planned launch point. Weather conditions were terrible. The sea had thirty-foot waves, and the planes faced a strong headwind to Japan and China. Most of the men decided they were on a suicide mission, and for some it was.

Fortunately, the headwind changed to a tailwind, which enabled some of the planes to reach the China coast after they dropped their bombs on Japan. All the bombers completed their mission over Japan and flew toward China. Some of the crews parachuted or landed in China, some crash-landed on the mainland, and some ditched at sea.

When the raid was reported in the States, the morale of Americans was lifted considerably. This was the first good news Americans had received after five months of bitter disappointments. The physical damage to Japan was small, but the psychological effect in America was huge. President Roosevelt, who had a gift for feeling the public's pulse, announced the planes came from "Shangri-La." It was reported in the American press that the raid infuriated Emperor Hirohito and the Japanese military. As a result, the Japanese military slaughtered 250,000 Chinese in three months as they searched and captured the Americans and killed anyone who had assisted them.

I left UGA on July 1, 1943, and did not return as a student until 1947 to complete my college education to earn my degree.

THE GEORGIA-U.C.L.A. ROSE BOWL GAME

A Brilliant Crowd---A Thrilling Game

THEY CAME, THEY SAW, THEY LOST

The sponsors of Alabama's Crimson Tide made a colorful showing at the classic game of the football season, only to see their team suffer a 21-10 defeat at the hands of Georgia's Bulldogs. Left to right are: Mrs. Babs Roberts, Richard Roberts, Gaydeane Castleberry and Robert Parrish.

THE ARMY CAME OUT TO ROOT FOR . . . ANYBODY

The Army, always ready for a good fight, turned out in force to see the game. They cheered both sides at every single play. The soldier in the foreground (right) must be an alumnus of one of the schools by the way he reacts to a good play.

GLORY, GLORY TO OLD GEORGIA!

Georgia's cheermasters (and mistresses) were Curtis Bell, Martha Sullivan, Jim Turner and Chief Cheer Leader Beverly Landford.

BEAUTY AND THE BEAST

Miss Kathryn Rice supplied the one and Georgia's Bulldog mascot furnished the other.

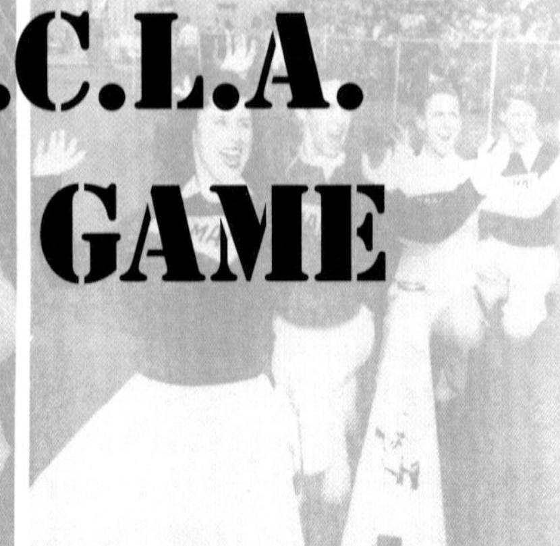

THEY CHEERED IN VAIN FOR THE TIDE

These are the Alabama cheer leaders: Alice Crittenden, Ervin Wyatt, Jimmy Carnwright, and head cheer leader, Peck Baird . . . Rah! Rah! 'Bama.

'BAMA'S BAND ENTERTAINED THE CUSTOMERS WITH A MUSICAL SHOW BETWEEN THE HALVES

ALABAMA'S PREXY WAS ON HAND FOR THE GAME

THE GEORGIA-U.C.L.A. ROSE BOWL GAME

Chapter 5

The 1942 Georgia football team won the Rose Bowl game 9 – 0. The game was played on January 1, 1943. The following articles and pictures that appear in this chapter are from the sports pages of *The Los Angeles Times,* dated January 2, 1943. Unless otherwise indicated, they and several other items will be donated to the UGA Archives.

[PART II.] 9

GEORGIA DEFEATS BRUINS, 9 TO 0

Los Angeles Times Sports

SATURDAY, JANUARY 2, 1943

The game that lives in memory of all Bulldog fans: the 1943 Rose Bowl game when the University of Georgia Bulldogs defeated the Bruins of U.C.L.A., 9-0. The Bulldogs' Charlie Trippi was one of the heroes of the day.

This is Lamar Davis, brilliant Georgia back, returning the opening kickoff from behind his goal line to the Bulldog 43.

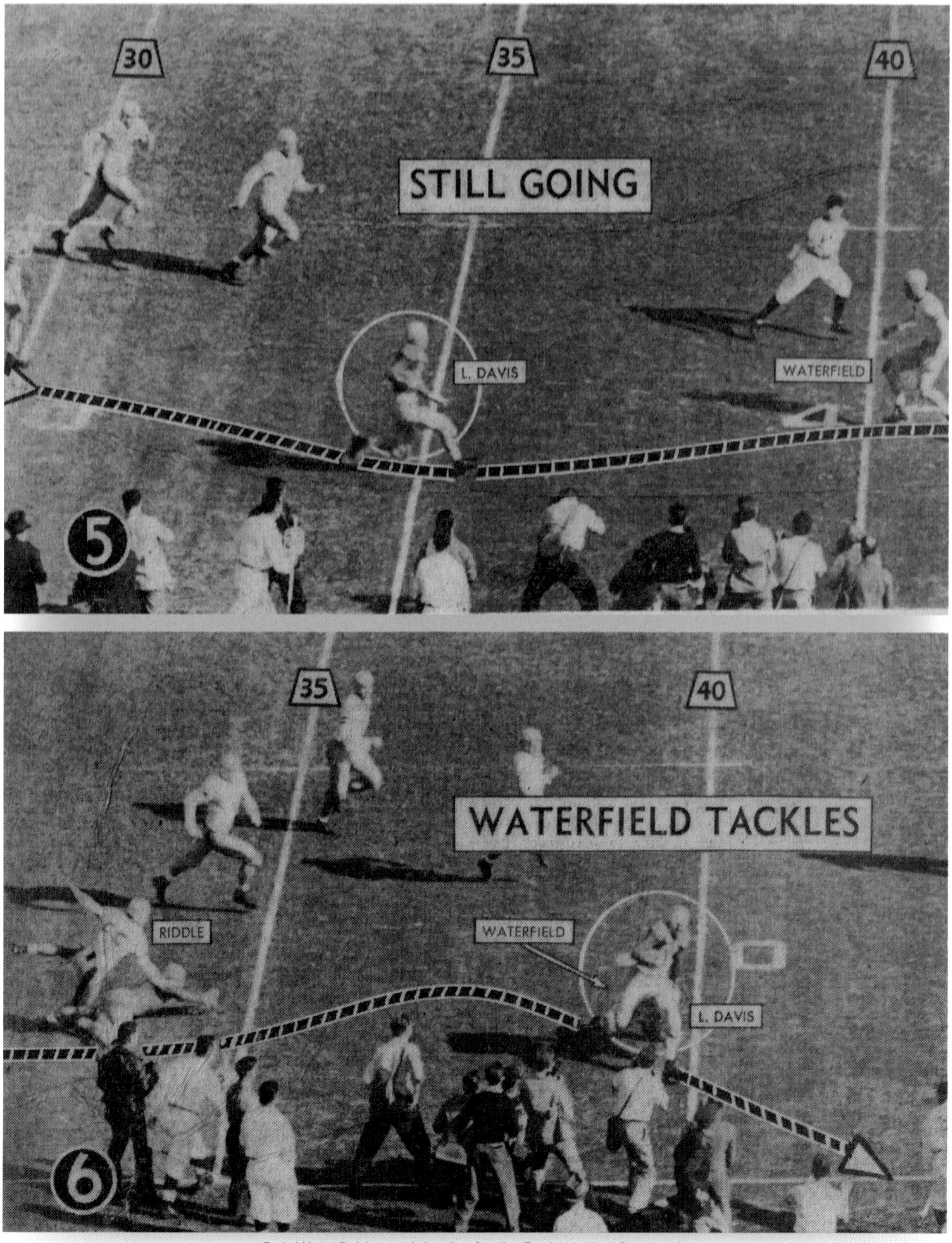

Bob Waterfield saved the day for the Bruins with a fine tackle.

GLORY, GLORY TO OLD GEORGIA!

Georgia's cheermasters (and mistresses) were
Curtis Beall, Martha Sullivan, Jim Turner and Chief Cheerleader Beverly Landford.

st	13	Tennessee	14	Texas	14	Alabama	37	2nd Air Force	13
est	12	Tulsa	7	Georgia Tech	7	Boston Col.	21	Hard.-Sim.	7

Georgia Team Called Great in Action Packed Tilt

Sport Postscripts

By PAUL ZIMMERMAN

You think directing a visiting Rose Bowl team is all beer and skittles, you should have worn the shoes of Coach Wallace Butts, the Georgia grid master, and made his rounds here for the 10 days prior to the classic that took place yesterday.

Personally, if it were our assignment we would ask the university authorities for a staff composed of a lawyer, social secretary, ticket agent, public relations council, bodyguard, chauffeur, private detective, valet and customary assistant coaches and team trainer.

TOUGH GUY

Doing it on his own, as this matured Georgian has done, how should be a combination of Chamber of Commerce, orator, movie and radio actor, politician, opera singer, psychologist and gourmand, and football coach.

Of course, a guy can turn his back on everyone, shut his ears to pleas, don a pair of smoked glasses, cut the telephone line and lock the world out entirely. If we had a Rose Bowl coach or ... did that. But Coach ... wouldn't be that kind of ...

When he stepped off the train at Pasadena a week ago Monday soon he announced his plat...

COUNTRY BOY

"First of all," said Wally, "I ... football coaching job to ...

"... I also want youall to be friends. I don't want to make ... mad at me. I'm just a country boy in the big town for the first time and I want to do the right thing—just so I get a chance to coach my football ..."

..., you can't hate a coach ... that. And he lived up to his word to the limit. If you ...

KICK BLOCKED—Here is Willard (Red) Boyd, Georgia tackle, blocking Bob Waterfield's punt on the first play of the fourth quarter. The ball bounded out of the end zone for an automatic safety and two points. Riddle is No. 22. Behind Waterfield is Poschner, Georgia end, who helped to rush the Bruin kicker.

Game Thrills 90,000 Fans

U.C.L.A. Considered Lucky to Keep Score From Becoming Rout

BY BRAVEN DYER

The chap who wrote "Georgia on My Mind" must have been thinking about the great Dixie football team which defeated U.C.L.A., 9 to 0, yesterday in the famed Rose Bowl.

Certain it is that none of the 90,000 exhausted spectators who sat in on yesterday's superthriller ever will forget the smashing sons of the South.

For sustained action there never has been a Rose Bowl contest to equal this one. Nine points ordinarily would not indicate much offensive football but the slashing Bulldogs came so close to scoring on at least five other occasions that the count might just as well have been 28 or 35 to 0.

BRUINS LUCKY

Seldom has a Rose Bowl team rolled up such a commanding margin in first downs (24 to 5) and yardage (373 to 159) and emerged with so few points on the scoreboard.

The Bruins can thank their lucky stars they got off as fortunately as they did.

Only their fighting hearts kept them in the ball game for three full quarters. In defeat, the U.C.L.A. fans can well be proud of the gallant stand which Babe Horrell's boys made yesterday afternoon. Nothing short of such dogged determination could have kept the score from mounting in to the 20's or 30's.

The Bruins were mighty fortunate, for instance, that those sprained ankles prevented Coach Wally Butts from employing Frankie Sinkwich in the same backfield with Charley Trippi except for brief moments during the terrific battle.

GREATEST COMBINATION

It was difficult to imagine what might have happened to the Westwood lads had Fireball Frankie been physically sound. I'll venture the opinion that Sinkwich and Trippi together, when both are right, constitute one of the greatest two-man backfield combinations ever to ...

Tennessee Overpowers Tulsa Grid Team, 14-7

NEW ORLEANS, Jan. 1. (AP)—Tennessee overpowered Tulsa, 14-7, here today before an estimated Sugar Bowl crowd of 70,000 but the Oklahomans got off to a fast start and staged a blazing finish that might have tied the ball game except for a last-minute ...

Eastern All-Stars Nip Western Eleven, 13-12

SAN FRANCISCO, Jan. 1. (AP)—A smooth-operating band of college all-stars brought the East its first football triumph over the West in five years today, edging out the Westerners, 13 to 12, in a spine-tingling charity game before a near-capacity crowd of 58,000 in Kezar Stadium.

90,000 fans rock stadium!

[PART II.] 13

Rose Bowl Contest Thrills Crowd of 90,000

Rooters Rabid During Game

Servicemen Plentiful in Massive Throng at Colorful Display

GOAL POSTS COME DOWN—Goal posts at the Pasadena Rose Bowl went tumbling down as a swarm of enthusiastic rooters raided the timbers following Georgia's 9-to-0 victory over the U.C.L.A. Bruins yesterday before a crowd of 90,000 who saw the Crown City gridiron classic.

Los Angeles Times Sports

SATURDAY, JANUARY 2, 1943

The Sports Parade

By BRAVEN DYER

Bruins Game, Atlanta Scribe Says

BY JACK TROY

Tide Smashes Eagles, 37-21

Postscripts

East Noses Out West, 13 to 12

Plenty of Passes but Only One Touchdown

12 [PART II.] ★

Mentor Horrell Praises Mighty Bulldogs

Trippi Lauded as Best Back

Bruins' Coach Says Georgia Best Team His Boys Met All Season

BY AL WOLF

As might have been expected the U.C.L.A. dressing room was no place to cure the blues after yesterday's Rose Bowl football game.

The players, dirty, sweaty and utterly exhausted, slumped silently to the benches as they filed in, stared stonily at the floor and, in some cases, sniffled a bit.

PASS OUT SMILES

But Joe E. Brown, the movie man who is a dyed-in-the-wool Bruin fan and whose business it is to make people laugh, quickly saved the occasion by bustling around to distribute back claps, handshakes and wisecracks. He even had to waste one on Mickey Rooney, who was wiping away a few tears himself while passing out towels.

Pretty soon everybody felt better and the talk started.

"You fellows have nothing to be ashamed of," Coach Babe Horrell announced. "You did a fine job and we're all mighty proud of you."

To the assembled press, he then continued:

"Georgia was the finest team I saw all season. They had lots of tricks and pulled them very effectively, they had marvelous downfield blocks, they passed us dizzy and also had the tightest pass defense we met all year. Yes, and they surprised us with exceptionally fine kicking. That passing reminded me of Dixie Howell and the Alabama team that played in the Bowl a few years ago."

TRIPPI LABELED BEST

Horrell opined that Charley Trippi was the best back U.C.L.A. played against in its 11 games this season — and that verdict got a quick second from the Bruin players.

"Most powerful guy I ever came in contact with," said Guard Jack Lescoulle, "and I mean contact, too. Wow."

"If Sinkwich had bad ankles," Horrell went on, "I'm glad we didn't meet him when he felt well. He didn't seem to have anything wrong with him when he ran, though."

Horrell refused to speculate what the outcome might have been if Bob Waterfield had got off the punt which was blocked for two points as the fourth quarter began.

WELL SATISFIED—Coach Wally Butts, center, of Georgia didn't appear very worried at this point of Rose Bowl game and neither did Line Coach J. B. Whitworth, right. Bulldogs beat Bruins, 9 to 0, in thrilling battle.

When all the world was young: Legendary Georgia coach Wally Butts, left, coached his Bulldogs to victory over Babe Harrell's Bruins in the 1943 Rose Bowl. Butts coached at Georgia 1939-1960, and was Athletic Director for much of that time.

Georgia Beats U.C.L.A. in Rose Bowl, 9 to 0

Continued From First Page

The ball shot out of the playing field for a safety.

Almost immediately the Bulldogs scored their touchdown with Sinkwich hobbling over right tackle from the 1-yard line. Leo Costa dashed in and kicked the goal that accounted for Georgia's 9th point.

A pass by Waterfield that backfired gave the Bulldogs their touchdown chance. Bob tossed the ball from his 35 and big Clyde Ehrhardt, the center, reached high and speared the ball, rambling 15 yards to the Bruin 25 before he was downed.

TRIPPI ROLLS

So sensational was the opening quarter that both teams threatened to score twice. And yet the goal-line stands of both sides rejected all touchdown efforts. The boys on both sides were so busy surging up and down the field that it was not until the second quarter that any punting was done.

DAVIS SCOOTS

Bruin backers groaned with pain when Lamar (Racehorse) Davis grabbed Ken Snelling's booming kickoff 5 yards back to the goal line and scooted upfield to his own 43 before Waterfield, the last man between the Georgian and the Bruin goal, pulled him down.

SATURDAY, JANUARY 2, 1943

Yard-by-Yard Account of Rose Bowl Contest

GEORGIA U.C.L.A.

GEORGIA BULLDOGS - ROSE BOWL CHAMPS 1943
GA 9 - U.C.L.A. 0

MY TOUR OF DUTY IN THE UNITED STATES MARINE CORPS

MY TOUR OF DUTY IN THE UNITED STATES MARINE CORPS

Chapter 6

I joined the United States Marine Corps in September 1942 in Macon, Georgia. All men who were between the ages of eighteen to forty-five were required to register for the draft and could be called to duty at any time. The only exceptions were men who had an official exemption, which very few had, or men who did not pass the physical exam. The Marine Corps V-12 Program allowed college juniors or seniors to continue their education until they were ordered to report for active duty in Officer Candidate School.

In an attempt to complete my education prior to serving in the military, I applied for admission to the University of Georgia and was accepted fall quarter in 1941. I attended the University of Georgia every quarter, including the summer quarters. However, on July 1, 1943, I received a letter ordering me to report for active duty. At this time, I lacked one course, bacteriology, and was unable to complete it until 1947. Fortunately, I returned to UGA, completed bacteriology, and earned my Bachelor of Science degree in 1947.

Approximately 160 students in the V-12 Program at Georgia were ordered to Duke University on July 1, 1943, for active duty. To comply with our orders, we left Athens by train. The passenger coaches were completely filled. Many of us stood or sat on the small platform on the ends of each coach. Several of the UGA players on the 1942 Rose Bowl team including Red Boyd, Bulldog Williams, and others were in this group. We and other students from Mississippi State, Old Miss, University of Maryland, University of Virginia, and various other colleges arrived at Duke. According to alphabetical order, we received our room assignments, our Marine Corps clothing, and our next semester's course registrations.

Most of the Georgia students had been majoring in agriculture, physical education, education, or some other less difficult courses. At Duke, we were required to take physics, mechanical drawing, naval history, and some difficult mathematics courses. Unfortunately, over half the Georgia students failed the first semester, were removed from the Officer Candidate Program, and were shipped to Parris Island to begin basic training. Although my grades were somewhat mediocre, I remained at Duke for another semester.

The Duke campus is shaped in the form of a cross, and the chapel sits at the head of the cross. By the side of the chapel in a shaded area were two or three benches which were seldom used. I sat on one of those benches and learned to study because I was determined to pass my courses so that I could continue in the Officer Candidate School program.

At the end of the second semester, we were ordered to Parris Island to begin basic training. We traveled by train to Yammassee, where we were met by drill instructors, who very shortly had us loaded on 18-wheeler truck trailers. These trailers resembled cattle trailers. Dressed in our Marine uniforms with overcoats, we carried all our possessions in our sea bags. The DIs kept shouting, "Now, close it up! Now, close it up!" This order was very difficult for us because we were wearing our overcoats and carrying sea bags on our shoulders. Finally, when the trailers were loaded to the D.I.'s satisfaction, we traveled to Parris Island. As we approached the island, we noticed a large sign, "This is where the difference begins."

After we unloaded at a receiving building, we were separated into platoons and assigned our quarters in Quonset huts. Two drill instructors for each platoon marched us to our quarters and assigned us bunks. There were approximately sixty men in each hut. Most of the orders we received were preceded by the word "NOW," which meant "immediately, if not sooner." We placed our sea bags on our assigned bunks and marched to the barbershop where all our hair was cut off. From the barbershop, we went to the delousing building and then to a Quarter Master building to be issued utility clothing, underwear, and boondockers. From the Quarter Master building, we went to the Armory to be issued M-1 rifles. Many of these rifles were still packed in carsmaline. We marched back to our quarters to begin twelve weeks of difficult basic training.

Reveille was at 0430. Twenty minutes were allowed for us to square away our bunks, use the head (or bathroom), shave, and be ready to march to the mess, or dining, hall for chow. A typical breakfast consisted of two pieces of French toast made of white bread covered with a sugar and water mixture, baked beans, juice, milk or coffee. The food was placed on a stainless steel tray divided into sections. Often the French toast and beans were in the same section. We were ordered to hold our arms at a ninety-degree angle with our arms from the elbows to the hands placed on each side of the tray, so that the men on K.P. could place the food on our trays as we walked down the serving line.

Lunch, consisting of a couple of vegetables, one meat, bread, and water or lemonade, was served at 1130. Supper, consisting of one meat, one vegetable, bread, water, or tea, was served at 1630. The food, especially the hash browns and mashed potatoes, was generally tasty. Because the basic training was so challenging, I assume most any food would have tasted good.

For twelve weeks of basic training, every minute of every day was planned and enforced by the drill instructors. The minute we crossed the bridge onto Parris Island, recruits learned quickly that the concept of "I, me, myself" was nonexistent and that the words "we and us" would be used. This was an important part of the mental training to force us to depend on the platoon as a unit. Basically, individual preferences and rights were sacrificed for the platoon and the Corps. If one member of the platoon made mistakes, most likely, the whole platoon was punished.

Usually, late in the afternoon, the DIs ordered us to "fall out" and get into platoon formation on the company street for close order drill and the manual of arms drill with our M-1 rifles. The uniform of the day was boondockers or shoes, utility uniforms, and pith helmets. The pith helmets were made of a hard material and sounded like metal hitting metal if the rifle touched them. At that time of the day, the sand fleas came out in force. The DIs ordered us to stand at attention and present arms. Knowing that the sand fleas would be crawling in our eyes, ears, and noses and biting us, they turned their backs on the platoon. The bites of the sand fleas felt like horsefly bites, and it was very difficult for us to avoid swatting the sand fleas. Even though we were standing at attention, invariably as some "knucklehead" moved, his rifle touched his helmet and made a noise. When the DI heard the sound, he ordered us to continue at attention and present arms for an additional ten minutes. As our rifles grew heavier and heavier, it was extremely difficult for us to remain in the present arms position. Consequently, if a recruit dropped his rifle, he was ordered to sleep on his bunk all night with the rifle placed across the bunk. There were also individual consequences if a recruit made repeated mistakes in close order drill, was late for a formation, or broke other rules. Normally, the punishment was several dozen pushups or sit-ups or some type of other exhausting physical exercise. Another lesson a recruit learned very quickly was that no excuses were acceptable.

On days when the rain was extremely heavy, we attended classes in the Quonset huts on Marine Corps history, nomenclature of various weapons, the appropriate method of weapon care, and the table of organization.

Toward the end of the training period, we moved to barracks at the rifle range for one week's training in firing the M-1 rifle. We learned how to fire properly from the standing, kneeling, and prone position prior to firing the rifle at various distances from the target. It is my understanding that the Marine Corps is the only branch of service requiring recruits to fire a rifle up to five hundred yards from the target. If a recruit continually missed the whole target, which was referred to as "Maggie's Drawers," he was transferred to repeat rifle range training. At the conclusion of training on the rifle range, we returned to our original quarters and resumed the type of training we had prior to duty on the rifle range.

At the conclusion of the twelve weeks of basic training, we and several hundred other recruits participated in the graduation parade and were called Marines for the first time. After that time, all Marines know "once a Marine, always a Marine."

After graduation from Basic School and becoming Marines, we were ordered to duty at Camp Lejeune, North Carolina, where the basic training was more advanced and more difficult. We were housed in brick buildings divided into bays with bunk beds. Each bay housed approximately fifty men. We were instructed

First Marines Assume Duties Inside Tientsin

TIENTSIN, China, Sept. 30 – (AP) – The U. S. First Marine Division entered Tientsin today to assume police duties in northern China's political hotspot, where Chinese Nationalists and Communists are at bayonet points and a Japanese army is yet to surrender and be disarmed.

Cheering, flag-waving Chinese lined the banks of the Hai River as the leatherneck division, which had won glory at Guadalcanal, Palau and Okinawa, moved 28 miles upstream from Taku.

The Marines, charged with assisting Generalissimo Chiang Kai-Shek's Nationalist troops in Disarming 250,000 Japanese troops in North China, were put ashore at Taku by Vice Adm. D. E. Barbey's Seventh Amphibious Force.

TOUGH ASSIGNMENT

Pending the arrival of Nationalist forces strong enough to take full control of the area, the Marines, aside from helping remove the stingers from a Nipponese army which is arrogantly aware of the fact it has never been defeated in battle, will undertake the following chores:

Liberate and give comfort to 2,900 Allied prisoners of war and civilian internees; keep an eye on 232,000 Chinese puppet troops between the Yangtze River and the great wall; arrest war criminals; guard and care for 200,000 Japanese civilians who had moved into the area since the Nippones aggression of 1937, and protect United States nationals, property and records.

The end of the war has brought little peace or security to North China. In the past six weeks there have been pitched battles between Japanese regulars supported by Chinese puppet troops and well-armed "Palu" units purporting to be soldiers of the Chinese Communist Eighth Route Army.

CLASH RECALLED

In one clash near the Tientsin race course two weeks after hostilities presumably ceased, Japanese tanks and artillery fired for 40 minutes before the Palu withdrew.

Trans have been fired upon and rerailed and looted. Bridges have been blown up and railroad tracks dynamited. The main line between Tientsin and Shanghai is so badly disrupted it has been impossible to send some 1,500 civilian internees from the Weihsien camp in Shantung province either to Shanghai or Tientsin by rail.

MARINES MOVE TO PROTECT RAIL LINES IN CHINA

Heavily-armed American Marines deployed along the main railway lines of North China today and rode guard on freight trains to halt an increasingly-serious outbreak of "bandit" attacks on coal and supply enroute to Shanghai.

Marine commanders ordered the Leathernecks out on grounds of military necessity after Shanghai's coal supplies had dwindled to the point where the municipal power services faced a shutdown within the next two weeks.

Thirteen American, British and Japanese freighters have been diverted from Chingwangto to Shanghia with coal supplies, but unless the railway lines to the mines in the interior are kept open, Shanghai's vital port facilities may be paralyzed.

Shanghai at present is the main base of operations for American forces in China and it is the port through which U. S. troops will be moved home.

Marine spokesman revealed that the rail lines running to the Tangshan and Kuyah coal mines have been cut repeatedly in recent weeks and that trains have been fired upon by marauding bands.

Chinese Communists, puppet troops and armed Japanese irregulars all are known to be in the area. as well as many well-organized bandit gangs.

Tientsin Warms Up to Marines

TIENTSIN–In this cradle of the Pacific war, U. S. Marines are finding a land of ageless history, deep satisfaction – and a future of promise, says Staff Sergeant Bill Ross, Marine correspondent for N. E. A. Service.

The city is beginning to warm up to the Marines, many of whom are, for the first time in more than two years' duty in the Pacific, finding "liberty sport" here. It is nothing like the U. S. – but it has the ring of a pleasure paradise compared to some of the former battle stations.

And the Chinese, always friendly to Americans, are convincing the Leathernecks that the best passport they can have is:

"Chan chu – I am an American."

---

more in squad, platoon, and company tactics, and fire and movement.

One major improvement was liberty on weekends. The physical training was intense in a very sandy and dusty area. There were days when the dust was so heavy that we could not see the man next to us. Lt. Callahan was our platoon leader. He was about 6 feet 5 inches tall, lean and in good physical condition. Lt. Callahan had long legs and probably could have hiked all day without getting tired.

The training at LeJeune lasted about three months. Near the end of this training, we made our first amphibian landing. With full backpacks weighing approximately sixty pounds, we hiked from our barracks to Onslow Beach, a distance of about ten miles. When we arrived at the beach, we loaded aboard amphibian tractors and were carried out into the Atlantic Ocean a short distance, turned around, and headed back to the beach. The driver of the Amtrak stopped a short distance from the beach, dropped the front ramp, and our platoon was ordered to move out. The water was about waist deep until we reached the beach. We immediately attacked to achieve the objective and were ordered to hike the ten miles back to our quarters on the base.

Furthermore, part of the plan was for us to run the obstacle course when we returned to base. Our utility clothing was almost stiff, and our bodies were irritated, especially in the crotch area because we had waded through salt water to reach the beach.

The last obstacle on the course was for us to swing on a rope across a body of water about thirty yards wide. With the full wet backpacks, rifles, hiking fatigue, and salt water irritation, half the platoon could not swing across the thirty yards and fell into the water. These men were ordered to return the following day to complete the course if they wanted to continue in the Officer Candidate School program.

At the conclusion of the training at Camp Lejeune, we were ordered to Officer Candidate School at Quantico, Virginia, for three months of additional training to include detailed studies of close order drill, map reading, small weapons, leadership, night combat, enemy capabilities, and tactics. Many of the excellent instructors were veterans from the Guadalcanal campaign who had first-hand experience in fighting the Japanese. One of the final tests required us to receive a map of the Quantico area and a compass from the instructors, be transported a few miles out into the boondocks at night, and then find our way back to the base.

At the conclusion of the training in Quantico and after passing all the courses, we were commissioned as Second Lieutenants and ordered to Reserve Officers School for approximately three months of additional training. The courses were similar to those in Officer Candidate School, but those devoted to leadership of Marines in and out of combat were more advanced.

The day my class graduated from Reserve Officers School, I had an emergency appendectomy and did not participate in the graduation exercises. After leaving the hospital, I had various types of duty until the next class graduated. As a result, I spent much time in Washington, D.C., visited many of the historical sites, and enjoyed liberty in the capital.

When the next class graduated in December 1944, I was given a two-week leave with orders to report to Camp Pendleton, California, on January 1, 1945. At Camp Pendleton, I lived in a Quonset hut at Tent City #2, which was approximately five miles from the Coastal Highway from Los Angeles to San Diego. The closest town was Oceanside, California, which had only a few stores—mainly a donut shop and a gift shop. On weekends when we were not on duty, we walked out to Oceanside on the Coastal Highway and thumbed a ride to L.A. or San Diego. Several of my friends and I had a standing reservation at the Biltmore Hotel in L.A. or at a hotel in San Diego. Normally, we had a planned date or arranged a date after we arrived in the city. We enjoyed evenings at the Biltmore Bowl or Coconut Grove, where many of the movie stars visited and entertained the service men and women.

To be assured of having a ride on weekends, two other officers and I decided to go to L.A. one weekend to purchase a vehicle. We made the trip, but we could not locate a passenger automobile. Consequently, we purchased a hearse. We charged passengers two dollars for a round trip to L.A. or San Diego.

Each officer had been issued a two-gallon bucket to be used for bathing, shaving, and washing clothes, so the passengers brought along their buckets to use as seats. I have often wondered whether this is how the term “bucket seat” was coined.

We carried ten passengers in the back of the hearse, so financially we were doing well. I learned that others used the same plan later. On May 30, 1944, when we were told we would be going overseas in two weeks, we sold the hearse for more money than we had originally paid for it.

On April 12, 1944, we packed our gear in a sea bag and joined a convoy for transportation to San Diego. As I was going up the gangplank to board the ship, I heard an announcement that President Franklin Roosevelt had died at Warm Springs, Georgia. All activity stopped for a few minutes of complete silence in the dock area. Shortly, all hands resumed their normal activities.

I bunked in Officers' Quarters, but I was responsible for a ship company of two hundred Marines. The *Admiral Hughes* was a converted luxury cruise ship which carried six thousand Marines. We were told the ship could outrun Axis submarines; therefore, we had no escort for transportation. We were scheduled to have liberty call in Hawaii. Two days before we arrived in Hawaii, two Marines developed spinal meningitis. Therefore, all personnel were quarantined.

After a short stop at Pearl Harbor, we noticed extra activity as we approached the Equator. We were told by the "Old Salts," men who had several years in the Corps, that we were entering King Neptune's domain and that he did not look kindly on interlopers. Unless interlopers had the proper credentials, King Neptune would react accordingly. Those who had previously crossed the Equator were called "Shellbacks"; those who had not crossed were called lowly "Pollywogs." The Shellbacks advised the Pollywogs how severely King Neptune punished the newcomers and even indicated that some would be thrown overboard. Finally, all the Pollywogs were assembled on deck to await the arrival of King Neptune and his royal party. When he arrived, all the Pollywogs completed the initiation ceremonies to become Shellbacks. After the initiation was completed, we were issued the proper credentials.

We proceeded to Guam for approximately two weeks ashore and to Saipan for a few hours before proceeding to Okinawa for combat duty. We landed on the beach near Kadina Airbase and bivouacked there for a couple of days before we went to the front line for assignment to the various Marine units. Four other officers and I were assigned to the First Marines.

I was ordered to be the platoon leader for an 81 MM Mortar platoon Headquarters Company, Third Battalion. The previous platoon leader, Lt. Murphy, had been wounded and was recuperating in a hospital on another island. Lt. Red Haggerty, who was the

"81" M.M. Mortar Platoon; Beall is second from the right on the top row.

platoon leader on Pelileu and for a short time on Okinawa, took command of the platoon when Lt. Murphy was wounded. I relieved Lt. Hagerty. The platoon had been withdrawn from the combat line for reorganization due to the number of KIAs (killed in action) and WIAs (wounded in action). The Japanese had lobbed an artillery shell into the platoon's white phosphorus ammunition dump where it exploded, killing six men, and wounding eighteen others. The corpsman was awarded the Silver Star for staying to treat the wounded even though he needed personal medical attention. My responsibility was to train the replacements who had been MPs or cooks and return the platoon to the lines as soon as possible for action. These men had approximately three days of training. Fortunately, the gun crews had excellent leadership and performed well.

The continuous rain during this time turned the soil into a quagmire. Even the amphibian tractors bogged. The only way for us to get supplies to the front lines was to send working parties back to the ammunition and supply dumps at night and then deliver supplies to the front lines. The quagmire was so deep and sticky that the men's boondocker soles were pulled off. Due to the clouds and continuous rain, the planes could not air-drop supplies for a short time. The fleas were a tremendous problem, and we had very little food. The fleas were acquired from goats and from the Okinawan burial plots where we went to get out of the rain occasionally and to avoid the Japanese incoming artillery, mortar, and small arms fire.

The burial plots were built on the side of a mountain and constructed by a circular slab of concrete approximately thirty feet in diameter with a small opening about three feet wide and four feet high. Under the cement slab, the natives dug out an area about six feet wide and five feet high around the edge of the slab with the center left intact with shelves on the sides and front. The remains of the dead were contained in urns and placed on the shelves. Each Okinawan family had access to a burial plot.

The 6th Marine division was on our right flank, and an Army division was on our left flank. The Japanese main line of defense extended across the southern one-third of Okinawa from Naha, the capital city on the west coast, to the city of Shuri, where Shuri Castle was located, to Yonabara on the east coast. They had well-fortified positions with advantageous tactical terrain and an estimated 100,000 troops. We were advised that Shuri Castle was the Japanese West Point, honeycombed with underground caves and tunnels used for hospitals, munitions storage, offices, and a communication center, and would be heavily defended. Later events proved this prediction to be correct.

High Bluff over China Sea - Curtis Beall in Okinawa awaiting orders after the Japanese surrender, August 1945

In an effort to get to the Japanese main line of defense, it was necessary for us to capture an area known as Wana Draw. The rifle platoons had tried unsuccessfully several times, but they retreated under smoke provided by smoke shells fired by our mortar platoon. It was decided that our men would use tanks in the next assault. The Japanese knocked out eight tanks as they entered the draw. The platoon covered the area again with smoke to protect the tank crews from Japanese machine gunfire as the men abandoned the tanks.

Two new sergeants joined the platoon. Sergeant Barrett was a former motorcycle speed cop in New York, and Sergeant Hobgood was a former professional baseball player in North Carolina. When the rain finally dissipated, we moved through the mud to set up the mortars on a range overlooking and east of the Wana Draw area. From this position, we fired many shells on Shuri Castle, along with artillery units and naval vessels including the battleship *Mississippi,* which fired sixteen-inch shells on the castle. When the first Marines, our regiment, was ordered to relieve the fifth Marines, we set up the mortars near the castle courtyards. As the weather improved, the planes made air drops of food, water, and ammunition.

The Okinawan farmers planted sugar cane and sweet potatoes on small cleared plots on the mountainsides. Of course, I enjoyed this abundant food supply even during the rainy season. Some of the platoon members who were not familiar with that menu learned to chew sugar cane and eat sweet potatoes. Even now, at our yearly reunion, some of them ask me if I still enjoy those food items. They act surprised sometimes when I tell them I still do. Sweet potatoes and sugar cane were better than eating C&K rations, which got wet and were more like eating wet and soggy bread.

In early June, after a few days at this location, we were advised that the enemy was retreating south. Our regiment was ordered to pursue them as rapidly as possible. As the rifle companies moved fast, it was difficult for us to displace the mortars to new positions and be prepared to fire. It was during this period that I received a minor gut wound, for which I received a purple heart.

As we continued south pursuing the enemy, we walked on a road that was more like a dam. On the left side of the road was a paddy field full of water and mud. Suddenly, two Japanese machine guns started firing from a hill on our right flank. We jumped in the paddy field on the left of the road for protection from the enemy fire. I crawled in the mud to the far end of the paddy so that I could check the men to see if any one had been hit. Only one man was slightly wounded. It was his second wound, so he soon left to return to the states. This was generally known as a "million dollar wound."

Even in critical times like this, humorous things happened occasionally. We had a platoon member, Fred O. Miller, from the Shenandoah Valley in Virginia. He had a red handlebar mustache, a silver tongue, and was one of the best at making "moonlight requisitions"—acquiring something without authority—whom I met in the Corps. He was supposed to be carrying a mortar base plate, but he talked someone else into carrying the base plate. When he climbed out of the mud, he had a case of 10&1 rations on his shoulder. At the time, we had not been issued this type ration, which was much superior to the C&K rations we had. He had acquired the new rations from an army unit on our left flank.

Later, when most of the fighting was over, Fred O. acquired two army jeeps. We used these jeeps temporarily until the battalion commanding officer informed the officers that the MPs and SPs were coming to determine whether the various units had more vehicles than they had been issued. When I returned to my platoon, I assembled the platoon squad leaders and passed the word that the battalion CO had given us. I was informed by some of the platoon members that the extra jeeps were driven into a cave which the Japanese had used as a hospital. A C-2 charge was exploded at the cave opening, which sealed the jeeps inside.

As the Japs retreated south, we fired many mortar shells set for airburst, which killed many of the enemy soldiers. The accurate firing was directed by George Peto, who was on the O.P. at the time. General Geiger, the commanding officer of the Tenth Army, observed the firing and highly complimented the platoon on the expert firing. Other regimental and battalion commanders who complimented me on the firing were surprised to learn that the platoon had many replacements who had only a few days' training and were previously MPs or cooks.

General Geiger replaced General Buckner, who had been killed while observing the enemy from an observation post with field glasses on the afternoon of June 18 at 1315. The Japanese fired an artillery shell at the outpost. The shell hit very close to the outpost and exploded on a coral rock, which caused the coral to shatter into small fragments. One of those fragments struck General Buckner in the neck; he bled to death in ten minutes. He was the only one in the outpost who was wounded. I learned later that he was the highest-ranking American officer killed in World War II. The outpost where he was killed was approximately one mile from our mortar observation post.

Most of the Japanese had been killed by this time. The First Marine Division in the center, the Sixth

Marine Division on the right flank, and the Army Division on our left flank, were ordered to set up a defensive line across the southern part of the island to catch or kill the Japanese stragglers who might try to return to the northern part of the island. Dressing as women and trying to slip by in a group of Okinawans or hiding hand grenades under their armpits or in their crotch, these Japanese stragglers were very treacherous. Inspections of a group wanting to pass through our lines required us to be very alert and cautious. The Japanese had done an excellent job of brainwashing the civilian population. As a result, many of the civilians gathered their children on the high bluffs along the sea and jumped to their death. Some of the bluffs were approximately one hundred feet above sea level.

Fred O. Miller had acquired a ten-by-ten-foot tent, which he gave to me. I set up the tent behind a high hill and a big cave. As I later reflected on these actions, I determined that this decision was dangerous. I gathered several sweet potato vines and made a bed under the tent, which was considerably more comfortable than sleeping on the ground.

One day about noon, I was asleep on the potato vine bed when someone shook me to wake me. I looked up and saw my brother, Fillmore Beall, who was an officer in the Fourth Amphibian Tractor battalion. I had not seen him for two years, but the first words he said were, "You are the dirtiest person I have ever seen." I had not shaved for several days, and the only place to bathe was in a bomb crater full of dirty water. His assessment was indeed correct. Needless to say, we were glad to see each other again and had an enjoyable visit. As he was leaving, he invited me to come over to their bivouac area on the beach so that he could take me out into the China Sea in an amtrack and scrub my back.

Shortly, the island was declared secured, so I accepted my brother's offer and walked about three miles to his area. We got in an amtrack, rode out a short distance where he scrubbed my back with soap and salt water. Even though it was salt water, removing the mud was a relief.

When we returned to their bivouac, I had a shower in fresh water. He also gave me a speaker from one of the amtracks. I did not see him again until I arrived home in March of the following year.

Years later, we had a supper club with several couples. My brother enjoyed embellishing the story of how he scrubbed the mud off my dirty back and made the China Sea muddy.

Shortly, the First Division was transported back to the northern part of the island to a base camp to be re-supplied with equipment and replacements. The camp was on a high bluff on the Motobu Peninsula. The civilians had dug out 110 steps in the side of the bluff to enable one to go from the top of the bluff down to the sea. The Corps gave us more than normal R&R to overcome the stress of the recent combat so that we could get in better mental and physical condition for what was an open secret—the invasion of the Japanese home island. Our division, the First Division, was scheduled to invade Honshu on or about November 1, 1945. Most of the men enjoyed swimming and collecting beautiful shells in the coral along the beach. The Officers' Club for the First Marines was an open area under shade trees on the top edge of the bluff with a few board seats nailed between trees and a few folding stools. After duty and normally late in the afternoon, the officers gathered at our club to discuss the events of the day and the current scuttlebutt. We also enjoyed listening to the current popular songs and news on the speaker my brother gave me. Some of the communications personnel had connected the speaker to the division communication system, so we had good reception.

Toward the end of July 1945, the arrival of the equipment and replacements was increasing rapidly, and the training schedule was returning to normal Marine Corps standards. Signs of preparation for another invasion were obvious. I distinctly remember on one occasion when marching my platoon to sick bay to receive tetanus and other shots, we passed by the Quarter Master area. The Quarter Master personnel had made hundreds of crosses which would be used to identify gravesites.

On August 6, 1945, late in the afternoon, while listening to the music and news at our officers' club, we were startled to hear President Truman announce that an atomic bomb had been dropped on Hiroshima the previous day. Russia declared war on Japan on August 8, 1945, and the next day another atomic bomb was dropped on Nagasaki. The Japanese offered surrender on August 10, 1945. A suspenseful four days passed. On August 14 at 1900, the Japanese accepted the Allied terms of unconditional surrender. The war against Japan was over. It is impossible to describe our exuberation and gratitude as we learned that the war had ended.

The commanding officer of Japanese forces on Okinawa was General Ushijima. He was ordered to prolong the battle as long as possible to delay the invasion of the Japanese homeland by the Allied forces. He successfully complied with this order until he committed hari kari at 0410 on June 21, 1945. Not only did the Allied land forces suffer from the loss of many lives and wounded men, but also the Navy suffered the loss of many seamen. Ships were sunk or damaged by the Kamikaze planes loaded with high explosives that Japanese pilots flew directly into the ships.

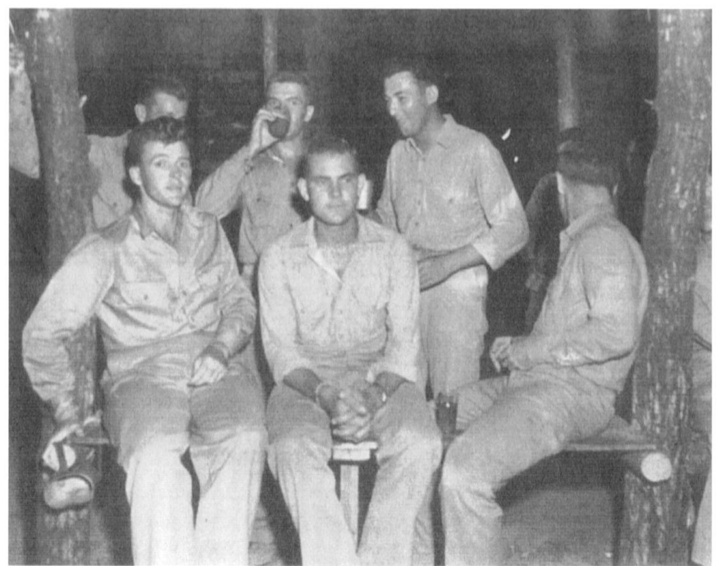

Opening of "Officers Club" on Okinawa after Japan's surrender. Lts. Barret, Beall (center front), Drum, Gibas, Kohler, Pucci.

It had been a year, and for some two years, since the men had tasted a civilian environment. These men desired to drive, to flick on a light switch, to see Burma Shave signs, to admire civilian cars, to watch children playing, to spend money, to drink a cold beer or a glass of cold milk. They possessed a longing to live in a peaceful environment free from worry about the regimentation, nit-picking annoyances, stress of combat, and priorities of war urgencies.

The First Marine Division had about twenty thousand men and was reasonably sure the division would be sent to Japan to participate in the surrender ceremonies and lead the parade down the streets of Tokyo. After all, the First Division had been in combat with the Japanese from the first combat at Guadalcanal to the last combat on Okinawa. The division had also suffered more casualties than any other division. However, General MacArthur, the senior Army officer, and other high-ranking Army and Navy officers and a few Marine officers accepted the Japanese surrender aboard the USS *Missouri* on September 2, 1945, in Tokyo Bay. The Army First Calvary Division led the parade through Tokyo's streets.

The Division received orders to prepare for movement to China. Consequently, the early part of September was spent in getting men and equipment ready for the movement. Even though they had formally surrendered, the Japanese had a large trained army in China. We were combat loading to take care of any situation. However, a typhoon developed and was supposed to strike Okinawa. Although we had not completed loading the ships, we were ordered to get underway immediately at 1500 on September 26, 1945. The thinking was that we would be safer aboard ship on the ocean than on land.

We were about halfway to China when we were caught by the typhoon. We were on an A.P.A., which was a relatively small ship; it was like a cork in turbulent waters. Periodically, the ship was in the bottom of the trough, and the battleships and aircraft carriers were at the top of the trough. In a short time, the situation reversed. The waves were huge and washing over the decks; everyone was ordered to stay inside. The ship rolled and pitched, so everyone got seasick, including the Navy personnel. The sanitary conditions inside the heads and other parts of the ship were terrible.

After about twelve hours of being in the worst part of the typhoon, we continued our movement to China as soon as the sea calmed. We arrived off Taku, China, during the night of September 30, 1945, and anchored temporarily in the bay off the mouth of the Peiho River. As the ships moved up the river, the riverbanks were lined with shouting and waving Chinese who had gathered outside their mud huts to greet the arrival of the Marines. Because we arrived at Taku during the night, the lights were out. Feeling apprehensive, we disembarked the ship in the dark. Fortunately, there was no opposition. The group of Marines for whom I was responsible entered a large warehouse on the dock that was a storage building for salt. We decided to sleep on the salt until daylight. The salt was fluffy when we lay down. As time passed, it became hard; by daylight the salt was like a cement slab.

My orders were to get the unit to the British concession in Tientsin, a distance of approximately forty miles, as soon as possible. There were no Marine trucks available, so we "moonlight requisitioned" some Chinese trucks. These trucks used crushed coal in a boiler on the back of the truck for power. Shortly, we had a sufficient number of trucks and shoved off to Tientsin.

We were amazed at the appearance of the area along the two-lane road. Practically all the houses were mud huts. The Chinese mixed mud, straw, and cow dung and packed the mixture down on a level surface of ground about four inches thick and let the sun dry it for a few days until it was hard enough to cut. They then used a tool similar to an axe to cut the mixture into blocks eight inches by six inches by four inches wide. The Chinese used these blocks to construct their mud huts similar to the way we Americans use concrete blocks in construction today. They did not let anything go to waste; perhaps this is why they survived under Japanese occupation. The Chinese even gathered the leaves, twigs, and limbs that fell from the trees.

Our unit, along with a few other Marines, reached Tientsin the first day. Other Marines arrived in the city by train and truck convoy the second day. The reception by the Chinese was almost beyond description. Their welcome probably out-shouted, out-shone, and out-smelled any welcome given to any other American troops during World War II.

The parade in honor of the Marines on the third day was spectacular. The wide streets were packed with civic organizations, schoolchildren, dancers on stilts, and musicians. All the entertainers wore bright colored costumes; some wore masks. Those on stilts did difficult stunts to the accompaniment of cymbals.

Our regiment, the First Marines, was billeted in the British concession and pronounced in Chinese as "Eng-Wa-Empoum." The billets had previously been occupied by the Japanese. Most of the musty, dirty quarters had no plumbing or heating. However, the quarters were a considerable improvement over what we had previously.

We were allowed to have a number one boy, basically a servant or custodian. I was fortunate to select one who spoke some English and who became an excellent employee. His name was Si-mung-ye. He and I had a good working relationship from the first day until I left China six months later.

My room, which needed extensive cleaning, was on the second floor at the head of some stairs. Si informed me that he was going to clean and paint.

A day or two later, I came back to my quarters after noon chow. As I started up the stairs, I heard an unusual noise coming from my room. I decided to stop to listen before I proceeded up the stairs. About every three minutes, I heard "plop." After a short while, I entered the room. Si had torn out the platforms where the Japanese slept on pads and had painted the walls and ceiling white with something that looked similar to whitewash. He had a five-gallon bucket of blue paint and was dipping a rag into the bucket, squeezing out part of the paint, and throwing it against the ceiling and walls. I had never seen such a pattern. I was surprised and amazed how attractive the job looked when he completed it.

Si, like many of the Chinese, was very thin; it was apparent that he had suffered from malnutrition during the Japanese occupation. I always took him a plate of chow when I left the galley after the noon meal. I observed that he always ate everything on his plate.

One day, I carried him approximately one gallon of rice, which appeared to be his favorite food. He did not like to sit at a table to have his meal, but he preferred to squat down on his legs and prop his back against a wall. He ate all the rice with chopsticks and did not drop a grain.

The second day after Si started working, about five days after we landed in China, I told Si I would like to purchase some silverware and silk. He arranged with one of his business friends to show us his goods.

The following night we traveled by rickshaw several blocks around some narrow alleys to his place of business. It was surrounded by a brick wall three feet wide and twelve feet high; broken glass was set in cement on the top. The entrance gate was a large heavy metal locked gate.

Si rang a bell on the gate; the proprietor came out to unlock the gate so that we could enter his place. I

U.S. Forces Near Junction In Bid for Okinawa Victory

GUAM, Thursday, Mary 31.–U. S. Tenth Army troops on Okinawa drove within 3,000 yards of a junction south of Shuri today and an American corps commander said the main Japanese defenses on the Island have been "busted" after 60 days of blazing battle.

"I think we've got them. I think the thing is busted now," said Gen. Hodge, commander of the 24th Corps, as the Americans hammered the last suicide outposts of Shuri, fanned out southeast from the captured capital of Naha and drove three and a half miles south of Yonabaru on the east coast.

Unofficial estimates said that between 5,000 and 6,000 uncounted Japanese dead still littered the crumbled ruins of Shuri.

Dispatches said Shuri was guarded only by a "shell of defenses" on the north. Hodge said he believed the Japanese had completely pulled out of Shuri and moved south, leaving nothing but suicide outposts in what was once headquarters of the enemy's Okinawa defenses.

Marines of the First Division, who broke into Shuri in a surprise thrust from the west, still were poised outside the crumbled ruins of the ancient castle at last reports.

JUNCTION IS NEAR

The Marine spearhead within the castle grounds reported enemy fire to the north and south of them was heavier than that directed at their own units.

Meanwhile, the Sixth Marine Division, conquerers of Naha, drove southeast of the Okinawa capital toward the mouth of the Kokuba river and reached within 3,000 yards of a junction with Gen. Arnold's Seventh Division in the area of Tera and Kamizato, south of Shuri.

On the eastern side of the island, the Seventh sent patrols 6,000 yards – three and a half miles – south and southwest of Yonabaru while other troops battled fiercely on the outskirts of Karadera, 4,000 yards southwest of Yonabaru.

The town was deserted two nights ago, but when the Americans attempted to move forward through it yesterday they met heavy machingun, mortar and some artillery fire from Japanese who had apparently taken up positions overnight.

Other troops also were held up by similar resistance northeast of Chan, about 3,500 yards south and west of Yonabaru.

6,000 Japanese Dead Litter Shuri Ruins

SUZUKI IS GLUM

Aside from these forces, the enemy apparently has few troops left on the southeastern end of the island.

(Radio Tokyo, heard by United Press in San Francisco, quoted Prime Minister Suzuki today as telling the Japanese people that the battle of Okinawa "is the deciding battle of this war."

("The fate of Japan and its peoples... depends on the outcome at Okinawa, which is rapidly reaching a climax," Suzuki said.)

An all-out assault against the remaining Japanese in Shuri apparently was being held up until supply forces could bring up reinforcements through miles of mud.

The mud also was holding up the attack of the 77th and 96th Divisions on the north and northeast sides of Shuri.

Our Attack on the Ryukyus

FOR TEN DAYS American naval and air forces, recently joined by units of the British Fleet, have been bombarding the Ryukyus Islands. The length and weight of the attack appear to forecast another powerful landing on Japanese territory. The Ryukyus stretch like a closely linked chain from the southwestern reaches of Japan proper to a point within 75 miles of Formosa. Together with that island they guard the approaches to the East China Sea and form "a perfect transmission line for airplanes and light navel vessels between Tokyo and the China coast more than a thousand miles away." Capture of the key islands in this group would give us easy access to the enemy's home waters and would cut the last of his major lines of communication with the southwest.

The center of the Ryukyu chain of Okinawa, which is supposed to be the chief objective of the Allied attack. Tokyo says that there are as many as 2,000 war vessels in the American-British naval force. These and other enemy reports are unconfirmed. But it appears certain that a great new stroke in our Pacific campaign is impending – probably an amphibious assault that will be mightier than that on Iwo Jima and that will carry the war much nearer to the heart of the Japanese homeland.

purchased several yards of silk for a few American dollars, but I neglected to buy an eight place setting of silver for forty American dollars because I was unaware of the value of silver. Although I had written my wife June a letter inquiring about the silver purchase, I did not receive her reply until three weeks later. Unfortunately, the price had advanced to one hundred and fifty dollars; therefore, I did not make the purchase. June's mother, who was an excellent seamstress, made June a silk housecoat and gown from some of the silk.

Shortly after Si started working, we agreed I would teach him English if he would teach me the Chinese language. After a few lessons, Si suggested, "We stop lessons." He was learning the English, but I was "no learning the Chinese."

The enlisted men in the platoon were billeted in what had been a theatre. The building was located very close to a high brick wall that surrounded the British concession and was topped with broken glass set in cement. There was a tree located next to the brick wall on the outside. Very shortly, some of the men got up on the roof of the building, stepped on the top of the wall, slid down the tree to the ground, and enjoyed unauthorized liberty. When they returned from liberty, they reversed the procedure and returned to their quarters. The only legal exit and entry was one main gate which was always guarded and required a pass for one to get in and out. These men enjoyed this unauthorized liberty until one Marine who slipped out was shot in the leg at one of the Chinese nightclubs. When he managed to get back to the "liberty tree," some of the men helped him up the tree and back to his quarters.

One of the platoon sergeants reported the incident to me, so I immediately went to their quarters to investigate. His explanation was that he was cleaning his rifle, forgot to check the chamber, and the rifle accidentally fired and shot a hole in the flesh part of his leg. To help confirm his story, some of the men had shot a hole in the deck, or floor. After he reenacted the accident, I stuck a pencil into the hole in the floor. It was apparent by the angle of the rifle, the hole in his leg, and the angle of the bullet hole in the deck that he was not telling the truth. Later, he admitted what had happened. Due to what the men had experienced on Pelilu and Okinawa, I did not make an official report on the event.

During the day in and around Tientsin, we were on patrol rounding up Japanese troops, disarming them, and transporting them to Taku for return to Japan. During early morning patrol, it was not unusual to see several Chinese who had frozen or died for some other reason on the street. The bodies were picked up by a Chinese crew, placed on a cart or wagon, and carried off.

One night about 0100, we were on a late night patrol traveling on a highway from Tientsin to Peking when we noticed what seemed to be woods on fire. The closer we got to the fire, the more suspicious we became. We deployed the patrol for combat and advanced toward the fire. We saw it was a cemetery with several hundred graves with a small fire at the head of each grave. Some of the farmers in the area informed us that this was an annual Chinese custom to keep the evil spirits away.

As I mentioned previously, the Chinese did not waste anything, including human waste. An outdoor privy was erected, and the waste near our quarters would fall into a box under the privy. Every morning a couple of Chinese would come by and dump the waste into a large wooden barrel called a "honey cart." The honey cart was then carried to the country and sold to a farmer to spread on the land for fertilizer.

Every country has its own customs and traditions; our customs and traditions are as strange to them as theirs are to us. One morning I was off duty and was in my room reading *The Robe*, a book June had sent me. I noticed a loud noise in the distance which grew increasingly loud. I walked outside and saw a Chinese funeral procession. Apparently, the deceased must have been affluent due to the number of professional mourners in the procession. Periodically, the mourners stopped and placed a bright colored pillow on the street, knelt on the pillow, and started mourning. The crowd also included musicians. Several musicians had cymbals, and others were on stilts doing various tricks. All participants wore brightly colored costumes. I was surprised that the noise did not wake up the deceased!

Not long after we arrived, we were provided Officers' Clubs, NCO Clubs, and Enlisted Men's Clubs located in various parts of the city. What a contrast this was to what we had previously. Normally, when we got off duty about 1700, we exited the main entrance and exchanged a couple of American dollars for Chinese

OLD GLORY RISES AGAIN *– Okinawa, June 9. – The Stars and Stripes fly over one more Jap stronghold as Lieut. Colonel R. P. Ross Jr., a Marine from Frederick, Md., raises the American flag atop Shuri Castle on Okinawa. The same flag was the first to be raised over Cape Gloucester and Peleliu by the First Marine Division. – AP.*

money. The Chinese moneychangers were set up just outside the entrance and gave us from 3500 to 4000 Chinese dollars for one American dollar. We did not count the Chinese money because it took too much time. The money was just stuffed in our pockets. The Chinese also expected us to bargain with them because they felt if we did not bargain with them, they lost face.

One night about 2300 when I was Officer of the Day, the corporal of the guard came running into the guard office to report that an unusually loud noise was approaching the main entrance. I walked to the entrance, which was about fifty yards from the guard office, to investigate. To my surprise, one of the officers in our battalion, who really loved drinking alcohol, was pulling a rickshaw with the driver riding in the rickshaw banging cymbals together each time the officer pulling the rickshaw took a step. When they arrived at the entrance, the corporal and I paid the driver of the rickshaw for the trip, took the officer to his room, and put him to bed.

The battalion commanding officer informed us that the Marine Corps and the Nationalist Chinese government were starting an exchange program so that five or six of the Chinese officers would visit with us and five or six of our officers would visit them to sightsee in the Peking area. Normally, one learned quickly not to volunteer for anything; in this case, I volunteered and was in the first group who traveled to Peking. I have always been proud I volunteered for this trip. We stayed in a palace and went sightseeing all day, every day.

Because Si had told me so much about Forbidden City, I requested that our guide take us there the first day. Completed in 1420, the palace was a vast complex of several villas, treasure houses, chapels, and gardens. It covered 178 acres and was surrounded by a 170-foot side moat and a thirty-five foot high brick wall. It was the world's biggest palace and had been the residence for twenty-four emperors. In these gateways and halls, the Ching and Ming emperors lived and governed China, which reached from Asia to the Pacific Ocean and from Siberia to the Tropics. They did not allow any unacceptable relationships, so all the male employees were eunuchs. There were several hundred rooms, which were as large as our present gymnasiums. The front of the main gate was on a very wide street. This main gate was called The Gate of Heavenly Peace, or Tiananmen Square. This is where the present Chinese leaders view the military parades and other ceremonial events.

Many regard Forbidden City as China's biggest tourist attraction because there are approximately seven million visitors a year. There are hundreds of bronze and other type sculptures in Forbidden City. One of the most interesting pieces I saw was a carved ivory sailing ship about six feet long with extraordinary detail; one could see the fingernails on the fingers of the oarsmen. The courtyards are stone, and the rooftops are a yellow mustard color tile. Many of the walls in the gardens were stone, and the ditches were filled with flowing water and stocked with goldfish. We visited Forbidden City for three days and saw only a small part because we decided to see other interesting places.

The next day we visited "Coal Hill," which was located across the square from Forbidden City. The hill had about two hundred steps leading up to a small building at the top. Being young and full of curiosity, we decided to go up the steps to see what was in the building at the top. We were somewhat surprised and disappointed to find a large Buddha as the only thing in the building.

We requested that the guide take us to a good restaurant for dinner where we could order Peking duck because we had heard that the duck was delicious. We walked down a narrow alley a short distance before we entered the restaurant. Located in the center of the restaurant was a rather large open grill full of burning charcoal. Over the top about three feet was a large metal frame with several meat hooks hanging down. After we were seated at a table, two waiters holding an eight-foot pole on their shoulders with ten ducks hanging from the pole came by. They requested that we select the duck we wanted by placing a knife mark on the selected duck. They then took the ducks back to the open grill and hung our ducks on the meat hooks to start the cooking process.

While the ducks were cooking, waiters served various types of nuts, spring onions, garlic, and chewfers. Chewfers were plants that look similar to nut grass which Georgians planted for hogs in the thirties. The waiters also served Sake and Chinese wine.

The ducks were ready after cooking for about forty-five minutes and were tender and delicious. The wooden tables had a round hole in the center where all the duck bones and scraps were thrown and fell into a box under the table. Several of the Chinese customers occasionally would belch. The guide informed us that belching was customary and that the loudness of the belch indicated how much the customers enjoyed the food. After some of the Chinese wine, we joined the crowd of belchers.

The next day after our visit to the restaurant, we traveled the road from Peking toward the Great Wall and met some camel caravans traveling to Peking from the Gobi Desert, hauling silk and other items. We soon arrived at the Summer Palace, a place where some of the emperors went in the summer. The residence and other buildings were arranged around a man-made lake, and in the center of the lake was a large marble boat. There was a continuous covered walk around the lake, and about every twenty feet there was a painted Confucius saying overhead. After leaving the Summer Palace and on the way to the Great Wall, we encountered a dust storm which necessitated our return to Peking.

The next day we devoted to visiting some of the other points of interest in Peking with a Chinese opera scheduled that night. As honored guests, we were seated on the front row. The first half of the opera was interesting and enjoyable because Chinese girls dressed in brightly colored costumes performed various difficult dance steps. The second part of the program consisted primarily of Chinese music, which was less enjoyable. However, as honored guests sitting on the front row, we appeared to enjoy the entire program.

The next day we loaded our gear in the jeeps and returned to duty in Tientsin. Later, another officer and I returned to Peking on a weekend and stayed in a Peking hotel. We used most of our time to revisit Forbidden City. In my opinion, Forbidden City is one of the Wonders of the World.

In Tientsin, several nice restaurants opened after our arrival. Some of the restaurants were managed by White Russians and by Chinese. The White Russians served mostly American food; their specialty was borscht, a delicious soup with a beet and cabbage base. One of these restaurants that we especially enjoyed visiting was arranged so that the diners would have a table on the second floor by a large glass window where they could watch a game similar to our handball game on the first floor. The Chinese name of the game was "we-lee-chew." The Chinese owners soon changed their menus to American-type food when they observed the White Russian owners were getting most of the business.

Unfortunately, I contracted hepatitis and was admitted to the hospital. The treatment was "nothing to eat or drink for several days—except hard candy and grapefruit juice." The medics drew several vials of blood every day to check my condition. The hospital was a large building with several floors and was full of other Marines who also had hepatitis. I knew of only a couple of men who died from the disease, but several were ordered to a hospital ship off the coast or back to the states for treatment. The windows in the hospital did not fit the opening; we stuffed paper and old clothes in the cracks to keep the cold air outside. That was the only occasion when I slept in my parka overcoat.

Most of the men were eager to return to the states, so the Marine Corps adopted a point system to return the men in an orderly manner. The criteria for the points were one point for each month overseas, five points for each Purple Heart, and several points for each campaign. The Marine Corps gradually decreased the points each month as new replacements arrived.

My magic number of forty-five points was reached, so I was advised I could leave when I was discharged from the hospital. I was discharged in early March 1946 and ordered to board a ship in Taku, China, where I would be the commanding officer for about three hundred enlisted men returning stateside.

After we boarded the ship and were ready to get underway, I assembled the men and reminded them that we had all weathered some tough times together and were now on our journey home. I informed them that if they would not give me any trouble, I would not give them any trouble. They apparently understood my advice because I never encountered a more disciplined group.

We departed Taku and did not see land again for eighteen days, when we arrived in San Francisco, California. I had never seen the Golden Gate Bridge. As a result of that experience, I now have a very clear mental picture of the bottom side of the Golden Gate Bridge and remember how good it was to travel under the bridge, go past Alcatraz, and dock at the San Francisco port.

Beall C.A.
USMCR

I departed San Francisco and traveled to my home in Brewton, Georgia, for a thirty-day leave. At the end of the leave, I was ordered to Parris Island, South Carolina, for what I thought would be to receive my discharge from the Marine Corps. Instead, I was informed I was being ordered to inactive duty and would remain in the Marine Reserves.

Each summer I attended two weeks of active duty at Camp LeJeune, North Carolina, to attend various refresher courses on tactics and table of organization. I was surprised to learn how rapidly things were changing.

At home in Brewton, Georgia, in 1951, I was attending to forty baby calves that I had purchased from some of the dairy farmers around Tampa, Florida. June came out to the barn and brought me a special delivery letter from the Navy Department, which contained orders for me to return to active duty and to report to Quantico, Virginia, to attend a Junior Officers' School. The United States was involved in the Korean War at the time. Those men recalled to active duty were well aware it would be just a matter of time before our troops would be in Korea.

A man in Macon, Georgia, Fletcher Hanson, was also in the group ordered to active duty. Fletcher Hanson had a thirty percent disability due to shrapnel in his lungs received in World War II. He and I rode to Quantico together; our wives, Margie and June, planned to join us after we located living quarters in Fredericksburg, Virginia, which was a short distance from Quantico.

Fortunately, we located a place to live, and our wives came to Fredericksburg about three weeks after we arrived. June and Anita, our first child, lived in an upstairs apartment with an elderly couple, Mr. and Mrs. Grey, who lived on the first floor. Mr. Grey had a productive garden located back of his house. Anita, who was three years old, enjoyed visiting him while he was working in his garden and visiting Mrs. Grey, who had difficulty in walking. Several weekends we visited many of the historical sites in Washington, D.C, which was just a short distance from Fredericksburg.

Fletcher and I commuted from Fredericksburg to Quantico daily and ate breakfast in a local restaurant. We both loved grits and ordered them every morning, even though they were not listed on the menu. The waitress surprised us one morning and served grits. Later, when our duty would not allow us to have breakfast there, over half of their regular customers were ordering grits.

There was a severe shortage of junior grade officers in Korea, so the Marine Corps ordered approximately eighteen hundred First Lieutenants to active duty to attend a Junior Officers' School for refresher courses in tactics. Upon completion of the school, which lasted about three months, these First Lieutenants were promoted to Captains.

About one month after the school began, I injured my back and became a patient at the Naval Hospital in Quantico. After four weeks there, I was advised by the medical staff that I had an abnormal curvature of the spine which caused chronic strain of the back ligaments. I would be promoted to Captain if I passed the physical test. Of course, I could not pass the physical due to my back problem; therefore, I was ordered to inactive duty again.

About three months later, I received my honorable discharge from the Marine Corps. Fletcher also was ordered to inactive duty and received his honorable discharge due to his disability.

I did not have any contact with the men in our 81 MM platoon until 1987. June and I had been on a Scandinavian trip with her sister and brother-in-law and had returned home on Wednesday. The next day June informed me that Bill Mikel, who was a corporal in the platoon, had called to talk to me. I was delighted to hear from him. He informed me that he remembered I was from Georgia and decided to call information in Atlanta. My son, Curtis A. Beall, Jr., who lived in Atlanta, received the call and gave Bill my home phone number. He indicated that the men in the platoon had heard that I was killed in the Korean War, which was obviously incorrect. He also informed me that several in the platoon wanted to have a reunion in Columbus, Ohio, over the weekend and invited me to attend.

I called Eastern Airlines, made the flight reservation, and arrived in Columbus, Ohio, in time for the reunion.

Traveling from the airport in a Harley Hotel van was another couple, Gilder and Helen Kelley from Eldridge, Alabama. Gilder was a member of the platoon and was going to the reunion as well. We recognized each other even though we had not seen or heard from each other for approximately forty years. Gilder was the platoon chaplain.

The reunion lasted for four days. How nice it was to see all the men again and to meet their wives. I was impressed, not surprised, to hear that all these men were involved in their community affairs and in helping others.

Since that first reunion, we have met for a reunion every year at different locations in the country: Washington, D.C.; Columbus, Ohio; San Diego, California; Oklahoma City, Oklahoma; St. Louis, Missouri; Savannah, Georgia; Branson, Missouri; and other places. Usually, we meet the first weekend after Labor Day, arrive on Wednesday, and depart on Sunday morning.

In 2005, we met in New Bern, North Carolina. Normally on Friday, we are invited to tour a military base in the area. On Saturday, there is a memorial service in the morning and a banquet in the evening with an outstanding speaker. One example was Major General Robert Flanagan, USMC Commanding Officer at Cherry Point, North Carolina, in charge of all Marine aviation operations east of the Mississippi, who spoke at the 2003 banquet in Savannah. Then after breakfast on Sunday morning, we all return to our homes.

When we first met for the reunion, approximately forty-five men attended. However, due to health reasons and the Grim Reaper taking his toll, we have only sixteen men and their wives attending now. Several couples now bring their children, who also enjoy the reunions. A newsletter is published about six times annually, and we communicate by telephone.

I was so blessed and fortunate to have such an outstanding and capable group of men in the platoon. If I had had the opportunity to select a platoon of men in the Marine Corps, I could not have selected a better group.

MY BUSINESS LIFE

MY BUSINESS LIFE

Chapter 7

When I received my Bachelor of Science degree with a major in Agronomy and a minor in Animal Husbandry from the University of Georgia in 1947, I was offered a civil service job with the Soil Conservation Service in Boca Raton, Florida. However, I decided to join my father in the farming business and live in Brewton. In addition to farming, I accepted a State Department of Agricultural Education position to teach a Veterans Agricultural class in Dexter, Georgia. I encountered a problem, however, because I had no car. Because all the auto plants had been producing military vehicles, the purchase of a civilian car was almost impossible. I decided to visit the Atlanta General Motors Company to acquire information about the purchase of a car. I met Mr. Sever, a General Motors official, who assured me that I would have a car within two weeks. Fortunately, within two weeks, a car was available, and I paid eight hundred dollars for it. Consequently, I have purchased General Motors products since that time.

The Government established a program in which returning veterans could enroll in a Veterans Agricultural class, attend class four hours weekly, and receive ninety dollars monthly. The teachers were paid \$225 plus mileage monthly. Teachers were required to visit the veterans' farms twice a month. This was a very popular program because it provided beneficial assistance to the returning veterans who were interested in agriculture. Of course, agriculture was our major economic business at the time.

The number of students enrolled in the class could not exceed twenty-five students. Very shortly, the number of names on the waiting list necessitated another class. Gordon Lord, a UGA graduate, started the second class.

After a few months, a group of East Laurens County veterans requested that I teach a class at Brewton. To qualify for these veterans' classes, a school was required to have an Agriculture Department with a teacher, a shop, and a canning plant. Brewton did not meet these qualifications. I met with this veterans group several times to discuss the procedure to qualify Brewton School for a Veterans Agricultural class. The veterans volunteered to move some of the barracks from Camp Wheeler, near Macon, and construct a shop and canning plant. Mr. W.H. Lovett volunteered to furnish some of his transfer trucks and trailers to move the barracks.

In approximately three months, the building was constructed, and the agricultural class began with a new agricultural instructor. When we began the first Veterans Agricultural class, the shop and canning plant equipment and tools were furnished primarily from Army surplus and the State Department of Education. When I resigned as instructor at Dexter, Roy Malone, a UGA graduate who majored in agriculture, became the instructor.

I continued teaching veterans and farmers until 1951. Due to the benefits and potential for advancement, I accepted a job with the Dublin Production Credit Association. I was employed with PCA for approximately fifteen months. When the manager of the Federal Land Bank, which was a part of the Farm Credit System, passed away, I accepted the job. The PCA made short-term loans, and the FLB made long-term loans of five-to-forty years on farm real estate. Two weeks after I accepted the job, the secretary of the Federal Land Bank was killed in an automobile accident. Fortunately, I knew a lady with whom I had attended school who accepted the secretary's job. She served as the Federal Land Bank secretary until I retired.

The Dublin Association was chartered for business in Laurens, Johnson, Treutlen, and Wilkinson counties. We had an aggressive lending and collection policy. As a result, our loan volume increased rapidly, and we cleared every loan payment for several years without a foreclosure.

In the mid-sixties, the district officials and the parent organization, the FLB of Columbia, South Carolina, decided to consolidate some of the smaller associations. Therefore, the Dublin Association absorbed the old Eastman Association, which included the counties of Dodge, Telfair, Bleckley, and Twiggs. Due to the increase in the volume of business in 1968, the construction of a new office building and additional employees were necessary.

A few years later, we purchased a branch office building in Eastman, Georgia, and staffed it with two

The Federal Land Bank Association office in Dublin, Ga.

employees to serve our borrowers in the newly acquired counties. Rick Towns and Mary Ann Moore were employed—Towns as the branch office manager.

In the Dublin office, the employees were Curtis Beall, President; Ed Kight, Vice President; Al Scarborough, Assistant Vice President; Mary Wade Edenfield, Senior Secretary; Jimmie Beacham, Assistant Secretary; and Velinda Stanley, Assistant Secretary. At that time, it was possible to hire the best qualified person for the job. As a result of that policy, we had one of the highest rated associations in the Third Farm Credit District, which included Georgia, Florida, North Carolina, and South Carolina. Three of these employees and I attended the same high school, and two of the secretaries and I attended Johnson Street grammar school in Dublin, Georgia.

Prior to 1970, the FLB had a separate appraisal section, and all land and building loan applications had to be appraised by an FLB appraiser. This was a cumbersome procedure, so the bank began to train and appoint various individuals in the association offices as appraisers. I was appointed an appraiser in 1970 and probably enjoyed the appraiser position more than any other phase of my job. This gave me the opportunity to get out of the office and to utilize information acquired from college classes in the study of soils.

Two counties appeared to have more than their share of "moonshiners." On several occasions when appraising the farms and walking over the land, I discovered whiskey stills. If the owners were making whiskey at the time, I usually moved to another area.

One of the most unusual situations occurred in 1975. We had an application from an applicant who is still living; therefore, I will refer to him as "John Doe." His farm was located on Highway 199, known as the River Road, which bordered the Oconee River. His land was a long narrow tract containing about four hundred acres. I decided to park my car on the right-of-way of the highway, walk the north boundary line to the river, walk south along the river until I came to the south boundary line, and follow that boundary back to the highway.

Because we had rain frequently that year, there were several wet weather ponds on the property. After walking around one of these ponds, I came to a two-story camp house. As I approached the camp house, two dogs barked and ran toward me. One of the dogs was a small mixed breed mutt. The other dog was a brown bulldog with a white face, one ear and scars, bloody face, and appeared to be a vicious animal. I had a hickory stick, so I was not too concerned about him getting too close to me. Upon closer observation, I saw a deer and two hogs hanging from a pole by the side of the camp house. Whoever dressed the animals had allowed the intestines to fall on the ground. The flies and odor were detestable!

Because I needed to see the inside of the camp house to determine its value, I knocked on the front porch of the house with my stick. When the front door opened, a beautiful blonde girl about eighteen years old, dressed in an extremely short bikini, a small halter, and silver slippers appeared. I was somewhat flabbergasted! I told the girl I was appraising the property for "John Doe" and that I needed to see the inside of the camp house. She invited me to come inside.

After I inspected the first floor, we went up the stairs to the second floor. In the first bedroom was a small pig with only his head uncovered lying in the bed. I was uncomfortable before I saw the pig in the bed, but I knew then it was time to finish my inspection rapidly and to move on - which I did.

I made "John Doe" a small percentage loan, which proved satisfactory. It was several years before I told the office personnel or my family this adventurous story.

THE COURIER HERALD, Dublin, Ga.
FRIDAY, OCTOBER 8, 1982—Page 16

Photo by Bo Whaley

OUTGOING PRESIDENT
...Beall addresses the group with his retirement speech

Over 550 attend annual Federal Land Bank meeting

By BO WHALEY

More than 550 members and guests attended the annual stockholders' meeting of the Federal Land Bank Association of Dublin Thursday night, enjoyed a barbeque dinner, won door prizes, listened to gospel music, elected two directors and said goodbye to their president who will retire Dec. 31.

The West Laurens High School Cafeteria was filled to overflowing Thursday night as more than 500 enjoyed a dinner of Sweat's barbeque prior to the annual stockholders' meeting of the Federal Land Bank Association of Dublin.

Following dinner, the crowd moved to the gymnasium where toasters, electric irons, thermos bottles, electric clocks and fishing equipment went to lucky ticketholders. A combination food mixer-blender, the grand prize, was given away at the conclusion of the meeting.

Entertainment before and after the business meeting was provided by a gospel quartet from Toombs County to the obvious delight of the crowd.

Leon Phillips and S. C. Cadwell Jr., were re-elected to two year terms as directors and the members heard a financial report indicating that $17,208,316 in loans were made in the past year.

The highlight of the evening came when all present gave Federal Land Bank Association Curtis Beall a prolonged standing ovation after he announced that he would retire as of Dec. 31.

Beall has served in the farm credit system for the past 30 years, 27 as president of Federal Land Bank Association of Dublin.

Outgoing president Curtis Beall retires from the Federal Land Bank Association to a standing ovation.

Due to the excellent job of the association employees, I was offered a job in the home office in Columbia, South Carolina, on three different occasions. After careful consideration, I decided to remain as the Association President in the Dublin office.

The association had annual meetings in which we gave the financial report to the members, elected directors, and conducted any other business. We served barbecue meals usually catered by Sweat's Barbecue Restaurant and gave several nice prizes to lucky ticket holders. The attendance at the annual meetings increased to about five hundred people each time.

The Farm Credit System is a unique and cooperative credit system owned by borrowers who control the system through the election of directors by local association members. The federal government is ultimately responsible for guaranteeing the payment of the FLB bonds. However, I am aware of only two times when it was necessary for the federal government to put money into the system: during the Depression in the late '20s and during the financial farm crisis in the early '80s. The federal government was reimbursed in a short period of time.

In the late '70s, the system was allowed to make rural home loans to farmers. These rural home loans were a great assistance to many farmers who needed better housing. We had needed this authority for many years. Farming is an enjoyable way of life, but it is not a way to make money. I observed that in the end most farmers have their land (which becomes a part of the men), their houses, and very little cash, or other assets.

We had an aggressive lending and collection policy. When I retired, the staff presented me with a collection of letters from some of the past due borrowers whom we had encouraged to make their payments. Two of the most interesting responses to our collection letters are on the next pages.

In 1982, I recognized a great need for realistic farm and rural home appraisals. On January 1, 1983, after working thirty-one years, I decided to retire from the FLB. At the time I retired, the

Cats, Rats, etc.

I do not know if you will be interested in this, but I thought I would mention it to you because it could be a real "sleeper" in making a lot of money with a small investment.

A group of us are considering investing in a large cat ranch near Hermosillo, Mexico. It is our purpose to start rather small with about 1 million cats. Each cat averages about 12 kittens a year; skins can be sold for about 20 cents for the white ones and up to 40 cents for the black. This will give us 12 million cat skins per year to sell at an average price of around 32 cents, making our gross revenue about $3 million a year. This nearly averages out to about $10,000 per day - exclusive of Sundays and holidays.

A good Mexican man can skin about 50 cats per day at a wage of $3.15 per day. It will take only 633 men to operate the ranch. So the net profit will be over $8,200 per day.

Now the cats would be fed on rats exclusively. Rats multiply four times as fast as cats. We would start a rat ranch right adjacent to our cat farm. If we start with a million rats, we will have four rats per cat each day. The rats will be fed on the carcasses of the cats that we skin. This will give each rat a quarter of the cat. You can see by this, the business is a real clean operation. It is self-supporting and nearly automatic throughout. The cats will eat the rats and the rats will eat the cats and we get the skins.

Let me know if you are interested. As you can imagine, we are rather particular who we want to get into this; and want the fewest investors possible.

Eventually, it is our hope to cross the cats with snakes, and they will skin themselves twice a year. This would save the major cost of skinning as well as give us two skins for one cat.

Sending a Check!

Dear Sir:

In reply to your request to send a check, the condition of my bank account makes it almost impossible, my shattered financial condition being due to the federal laws, state laws, brother-in-laws, sister-in-laws and outlaws.

Through these laws I am compelled to pay business tax, amusement tax, school tax, gas tax, light tax, water tax, sewer tax, sales tax, liquor tax, income tax, excise tax, franchise tax, pole tax, and telephone tax.

I am required to contribute to every society and organization which the genius of man is capable of bringing to life. Woman relief, Unemployed relief, The Gold Diggers Retirement, also to every hospital and charitable institution in the city, including the Salvation Army, Community Chest, Red Cross, Purple Cross, Blue Cross, White Cross, United Community Chest, Community Appeal, Boy Scouts, Girl Scouts, Cub Scouts, YMCA, YWCA, All The Way Stations for Wayward Girls, Boys Town, Boys Ranch, and dozens More.

For my safety I am required to carry health insurance, life insurance, fire insurance, tornado insurance, unemployed insurance, compensation insurance, and old age insurance.

My business is so governed that it is no easy matter to find out who owns it. I am expected, inspected, suspected, disrespected, summoned, fined, commanded and compelled until I supply an inexhaustable supply of money for every known deed, need, desire, or hope of the human race.

Simply because I refuse to do something or other I am boycotted, talked about, lied about, held up, held down, and robbed until I am almost ruined.

I can tell you honestly that except for a miracle that happened, I would not be able to enclose this check. The The wolf that comes to so many doors now adays just had pups in my kitchen. I sold them and here is the money.

Yours very truly,

Broke-ly

Federal Land Bank in Dublin had approximately sixteen hundred loans amounting to $61 million dollars. I started my personal appraisal business and found the demand for this service was tremendous; therefore, I had difficulty in fulfilling all the requests. After ten years in the appraisal business, I decided to close it.

Several auction companies were active in the area. Due to my previous experience, I became a part-time employee with Roy Holland Auction Company. I maintained an awareness of current land and equipment values and worked basically in the eight counties in which I had worked as a Federal Land Bank employee. I worked with the Roy Holland Auction Company for a few years and enjoyed the work and relationship until Roy Holland died.

The farm economy during 1982-1990 was in an unbearable financial condition. I had anticipated this unfortunate condition because most farmers had survived by utilizing as loan security the equity they had accumulated in their real estate in the past few years. Since row cropping and raising livestock were losing propositions, I decided to concentrate my time and effort on producing other crops. It was not difficult to see the impending agricultural crisis. I planted twenty-five acres of Christmas trees in the late '70s and began baling and selling pine straw from six hundred acres of planted pines, which had been planted in the mid '80 s. I still maintain this operation today and trust that my health will allow me to continue.

Curtis Beall's work brought him in contact with many famous people. Above, he is flanked by Norman Vincent Peale and by Dorkus Darr, wife of Robert Darr, president of the Federal Land Bank of Columbia, S.C.

At right, Beall is shown with popular singer Anita Bryant and Preston Stamps, president of the Federal Land Bank of Dublin, Georgia.

GROWING CHRISTMAS TREES, RAISING CATFISH, AND MAKING WINE

GROWING CHRISTMAS TREES, RAISING CATFISH, AND MAKING WINE

Chapter 8

While working for the Federal Land Bank, I was in the unique position to observe the decline of a profitable agricultural economy. I decided to invest in some type of agricultural enterprise other than row crops and livestock. I planted twenty-five acres of Christmas trees. U.S. Highway 80 runs by my farm, and I had a field which is contiguous to the highway and ideally located, from a marketing standpoint, for Christmas trees.

Entrance to Christmas Tree Farm.

The first trees I planted were Virginia Pine, Eastern Red Cedar, and White Pine. There was not much available information about planting, cultivating, shearing, and insect control. Consequently, I used a trial and error method for a few years. The first trees were planted in seven-foot rows seven feet apart. This placement of trees gave me space to mow and spray within the row and across the row to maintain grass and weed control. It gave the trees sufficient room to make the maximum growth.

Contrary to popular belief, growing Christmas trees is a year-round job. After planting the trees, the tree grower must fertilize, shape the tree to about a 70-degree angle, spray for insects, maintain grass control, and wait about five years before the Christmas trees begin to yield a return on the financial investment. The different varieties of trees have different types of characteristics, so it is necessary for the tree grower to adopt a plan to care for each characteristic.

The most popular tree at the time I started growing trees was the Virginia Pine. This is a tree that requires constant inspection for insects, especially aphids. The pine needles fall to the interior of the tree and make it necessary for a grower to shake the tree to eliminate the dead needles prior to sale. The limbs are rigid and capable of holding heavy ornaments. The pine fragrance is a favorite of many customers.

The Eastern Red Cedar was the second most popular tree and was easier to grow than the Virginia Pine. There was no problem with insect control. Once the tree had the proper shape, it was easy to maintain. However, the needles were difficult to remove if they fell on the carpet.

The third type of tree was the White Pine, which is a beautiful tree with a soft needle. It requires minimum attention, but it is difficult to grow in this area due to the climatic conditions.

A few years later, the Leyland Cypress was developed. The Leyland Cypress enabled many growers located south of the Fall Line to continue their Christmas tree business. The Leyland Cypress has soft foliage, sheds very little, and stays fresh and green for up to three months if it is properly watered and placed away from a heat source. The Leyland Cypress was soon recognized as the most popular tree grown in this area when it began to replace the other types of trees. Some of the other types of trees are still grown to satisfy a small group of customers.

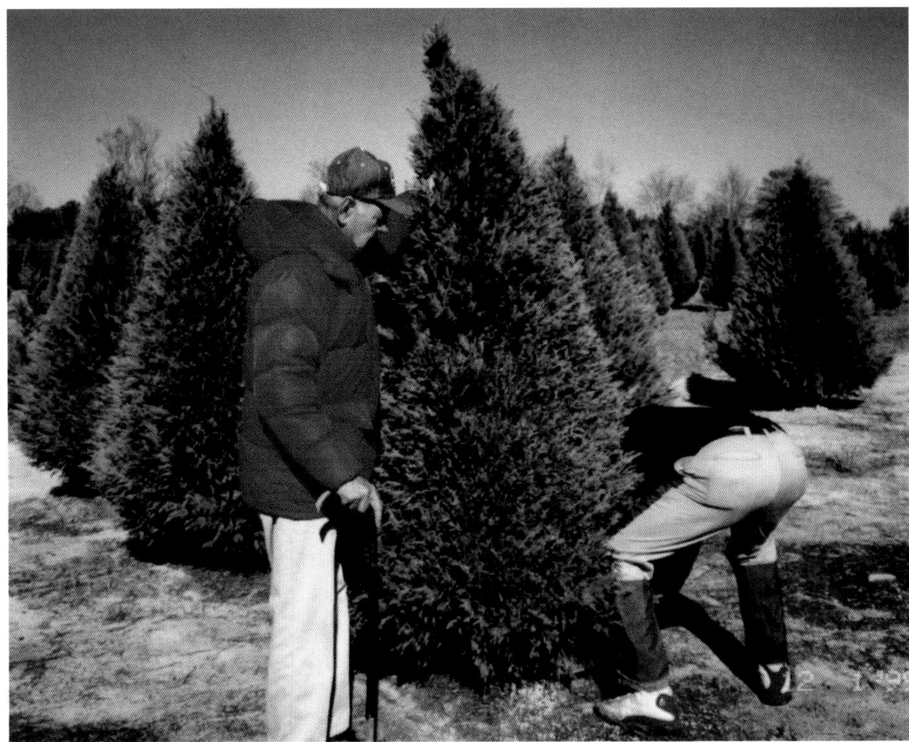

Curtis Beall helps a customer with a tree.

The business continued to grow, so I employed additional help. I had three employees to maintain the trees during the year and assist in sales at Christmas time. In addition, my niece and her husband, Mike and Kathy Sweat, assisted me at Christmas time and during the year to promote the business. Kathy and Mike knew many customers because Kathy was the East Laurens Middle School Media Specialist and Mike was the Assistant Principal of East Laurens High School.

Normally, we opened the selling period the week of Thanksgiving. When many of the families gathered for Thanksgiving, they came out to the Christmas tree field in the afternoon, located and marked the tree, and came back later to cut the tree. We had preprinted tags for this purpose, but some customers had their own method of marking the tree. We found trees marked with soft drink and beer cans, handkerchiefs, Kleenex, rope, cord, or shoestrings.

One morning as I was inspecting the trees, I found that someone had marked a tree with panty hose. I never did determine the customer's identity. I looked forward to finding who had marked the tree, but apparently, the tree was cut on one of our busy days, and I did not discover who marked the tree.

We had a processing building where the tree was carried after it was cut. The cut tree was placed on a shaker to remove any dead needles in or on the tree, a hole was bored in the base so it would fit into the tree stand, and the tree was netted to assist the customer in handling the tree. The tree was then placed in the trunk of the car and tied down or placed on the back of a pickup truck, ready for the customer to exit the field to carry the tree home.

It was amusing to observe the customers as they walked over the field to select their trees. "Courting couples" would spend considerable time looking for the perfect tree. The man was very patient as the lady walked over the field. We could normally tell if the couple was married. The first or second year of marriage, the man would cut the tree, place it in the car, and take it to the Christmas tree barn. After about the third year of marriage, the man would send his wife to select and take the tree home.

About 1990, several schoolteachers began to request a field trip to the Christmas tree farm. We made appointments for the children to arrive at a certain time to select trees for their classes. When they arrived at the field, normally on school buses, they rode around the field to observe the trees and went back to the barn so that their buses could park.

They then exited the bus, lined up, and followed the person in charge to a tree we had decorated prior to their arrival. They formed a circle around the decorated tree to listen to us tell about the importance of trees to our environment, the meaning of

Curtis Beall talks to children about Christmas

the various Christmas ornaments, and their religious significance. We also told the Biblical story of the real meaning of Christmas. Many of the teachers informed us that we could describe Christmas in a way they were not allowed to tell in the classroom.

After we talked to the children, they walked over the field and selected trees for their classrooms. We cut the trees and carried them to the barn for processing. The children stood in groups just outside the barn to observe the selected trees being shaken, holes being drilled in the bases of the trees for the tree stands, and watched us net and place the trees on their school buses. The children boarded the buses and exited the field to return to school.

The first ten years after we began this part of the Christmas tree operation, we had over 12,000 students visit the field. Unfortunately, in 2000, when my wife June suffered from a couple of strokes, I decided to devote more of my time to assist her. I sold the Christmas tree business to my nephew, Sam Beall. He and his family continue the Christmas tree operation.

Raising Catfish

As previously mentioned, I thought it best for me to discontinue the row crop and livestock business. In addition to starting the Christmas tree business, I began raising catfish for sale. There were three ponds on the property; two of the ponds were stocked with catfish. A year later, I opened one pond for public fishing and charged according to the number of pounds of fish the customers caught. After a couple of months, this fishing business was requiring too much time, so I closed the operation. The fish were so delicious that I decided to restrict fishing to family and friends. Through the years, we have really enjoyed serving and eating fresh water fish about twice every week. Also, our shut-in friends enjoy the fish each time we share the fish with them.

Feeding the catfish.

We closed our Federal Land Bank office at 5:00 p.m. every day during the week. After locking the office at that time, I traveled eight miles to my home, changed clothes, picked up June and a dip net, dipped out the catfish we wanted for our supper, cleaned, and cooked the fish. The fish were ready to eat one hour after I closed the office.

The men in our home office in Columbia, South Carolina, who might be coming to our local office for appraisal review work or for some auditing purposes, always called prior to their arrival. They never asked directly if we were eating catfish, but they tactfully hinted they would like to have fish while they were in Dublin.

The catfish, bream, and bass in other ponds are fed every day, so it is not difficult for us to get the fish we want any time. Several people have asked how much the fish we catch cost us per pound. My reply is, "I have not figured that and do not intend to. It might affect the way the fish taste!"

About every five or six years, we drain the ponds and restock the fish. The catfish have an excellent food conversion rate and are a sufficient size to eat after six months. The bream and bass are not ready until twelve to fifteen months after stocking. We have enjoyed the fish through the years, and I do not know a better way to relax than to "go fishing."

Making Wine

In addition to the Christmas tree and fish operations, I planted an orchard containing most of the fruit that can be grown in this area: peaches, plums, pears, pomegranates, apples, figs, grapes (seeded and seedless), and twenty different varieties of scuppernongs.

Due to the hot, dry weather we have in some of the summer months, the installation of an irrigation system in the orchard was necessary. The irrigation system is very simple and effective and can be controlled by one cut-off valve at the water pump or from seven valves located at the orchard. Each of these valves controls the water going to each of the seven rows in the orchard. There is an upright three-fourths inch plastic pipe with a spigot at each orchard tree or vine so that the water supply can be adjusted as necessary. The whole system utilizes three-fourths inch plastic pipe and fittings, except the seven cut-off valves for each row and the spigots.

The scuppernongs produced abundantly, so I decided to make scuppernong wine. Previously, an old timer who had made delicious wine gave me a recipe that I have used for several years. The delicious recipe requires these ingredients and procedure:

2 quarts scuppernongs, grapes, or blueberries
1 pkg. yeast, dissolved in ¼ cup tepid water
6 cups sugar
2 quarts lukewarm (tepid) water
Mash grapes and add other ingredients.
Stir with wooden spoon.
Cover with cheesecloth and let set for 28 days.
Strain into warm containers.
Put back into container, cover with cheesecloth,
and let set for three more days.
Strain again, bottle, and cork the bottles.

Several years ago, some of the officials and employees who worked in the Laurens County Courthouse had a Thanksgiving dinner, and everyone took a covered dish. Some of the officials had enjoyed my scuppernong wine previously and requested that I take a gallon or two of the wine to the dinner. Those who drank wine seemed to enjoy it very much. In fact, it was reported to me later that two of the secretaries in different offices burned out the carriage on their typewriters that afternoon.

Because one of the officials really enjoyed the wine, I carried him some bottles of wine separately for several years. His private office was located adjacent to his work area, and it was necessary to go through the work area to get to his office. I carried his bottle of wine in a shoebox through the work area to his office. After the first year, he did not request that I bring him wine, but occasionally he advised me that he needed to have his shoes repaired again. I knew what he meant.

In 2000, I started making blueberry wine by the same recipe, and many seemed to enjoy it as much or more than the scuppernong wine. My doctor recommended that I drink a small jigger of wine every night before dinner (supper). I was glad to comply with her recommendation, but I drank the wine about twice a week. The doctor enjoyed the wine, so I took her a large bottle about two weeks before Thanksgiving every year. When I delivered her wine, she stated, "The holidays can now begin!"

Normally, I make about ten gallons of scuppernong wine and ten gallons of blueberry wine every year and give it to others, but I keep a gallon of each for my own use.

A rare snowfall in Middle Georgia blankets the home and yard of Curtis and June Beall.

The Bealls' well-tended garden provides fresh vegetables and fruits throughout the growing season.

GOING BACK TO ATHENS TOWN

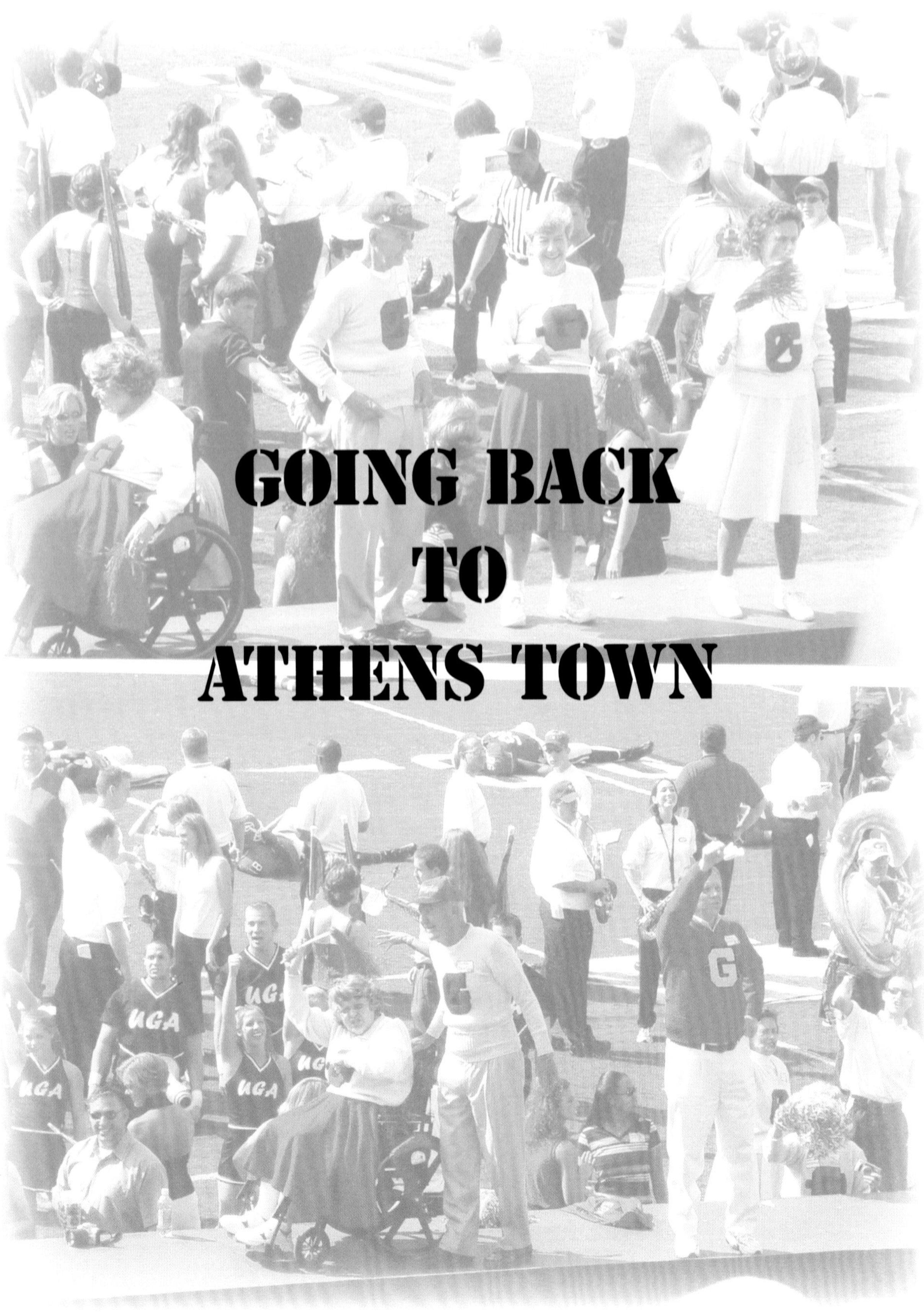

GOING BACK TO ATHENS TOWN

Chapter 9

YEAR OF THE "DAWG"

"Going back, Going back,
Going back to Athens town,
Going back, Going back to
the best old place around.
For the Chapel bell and
the Georgia yell
Going back to Athens town."

Curtis Beall and his granddaughter, Lisa Love, greet UGA VI at a Georgia home game. Lisa is a former member of the UGA Flag Team and Redcoat Band.

I had advised my family that I would return to UGA and turn a back flip off the cheerleaders' stand during Homecoming festivities as an alumnus when I reached eighty years of age. At that age, I still could turn a back flip off the diving board in my swimming pool at home. My daughter, Anita, called the Athletic Office, asked for information on my participation in the alumni cheerleading activities and the possibility of placing a trampoline by the cheerleaders' stand to catch me after my flip performance. She was informed that the alumni cheerleaders were not allowed to do any tricks. I was required to send them copies of my health insurance card and to sign a statement holding them faultless if I had an accident. I complied with their requests and have attended and enjoyed all the alumni activities since 2001. I had attended all home games for years but did not participate in the alumni cheerleading activities until 2001. Twenty-five members of my family have graduated from the University of Georgia, and my youngest grandson plans to enter the university in 2007.

On Homecoming weekend, the alumni cheerleaders have a special float in the Homecoming parade in downtown Athens on Friday afternoon and enjoy throwing candy to the children along the parade route. Some Friday nights we attend a picnic supper on the intramural athletic field where the RVs park and are sponsored by the Athens Motor Coach Club. On Saturday morning we usually have a short business meeting with members of the Booster Club "Cheers" and with current cheerleaders. Then we enjoy a luncheon two hours before game time. Inside the stadium, we lead the student body in cheers, lead the players onto the field prior to the game, and return to the cheerleaders' stand to cheer until the end of the first half of the game. During the second half, we walk around the field and lead the other spectators in cheers.

Setting up for the Homecoming Parade, the group takes a moment to have their pictures taken: (L-R) Alice Gilbert, Nancy Witherington, Curtis Beall, Louise Liddell, Vince Dooley and Dr. Bonnie Howard.

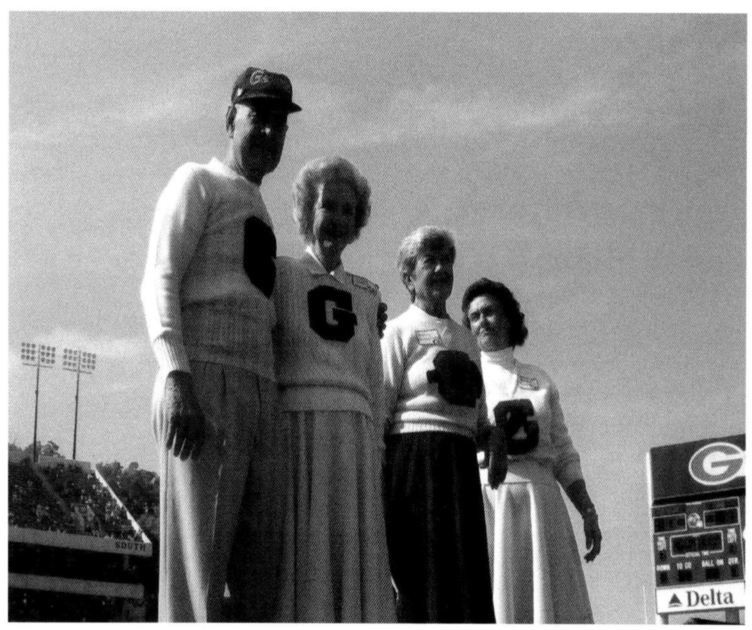

Ready to cheer for the home team.

I wear my original cheerleading sweater, now sixty-four years old, to the Homecoming activities. It still fits, though my family tells me it is a little snug. When walking around the campus prior to the Homecoming games, I am surprised at the number of invitations I get to tailgate with complete strangers. I guess this proves the old saying that a "Georgia man never meets a stranger."

Presently, I have the distinction of being the University's oldest, living, active, male cheerleader. My goal is to lead the Dawgs onto the field at the Homecoming games until I am ninety years old. I will review the situation at that time and maybe shoot for a hundred.

Curtis and wife June with son, Curtis A. Beall Jr., in Athens after the game.

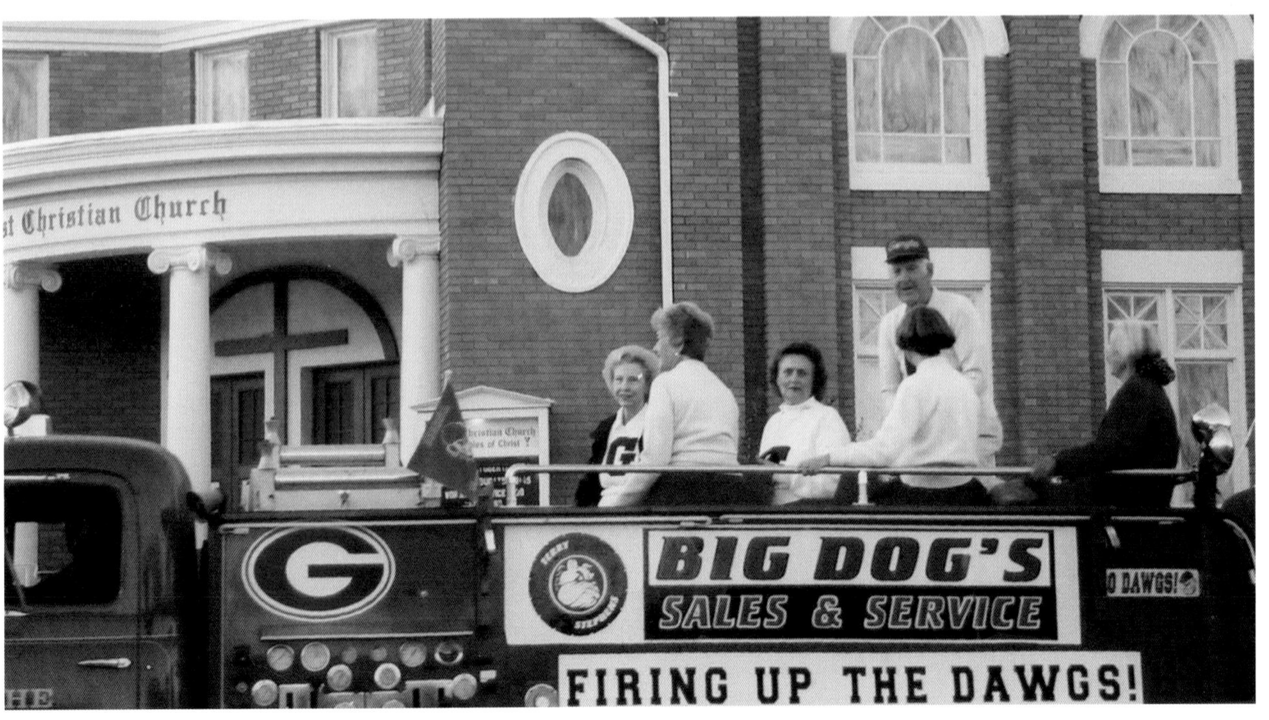

Firing up the dogs before homecoming game.

Curtis and his cousin, Lester Odachowski, also a former UGA Cheerleader, know that the Georgia Bulldogs are Number One.

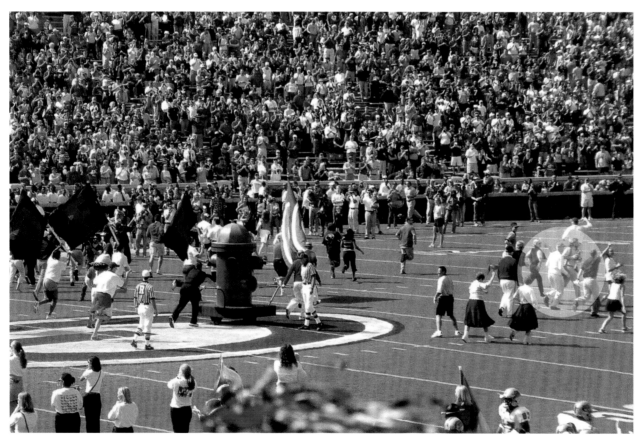

A sea of red charges the emotions and gets the fans going. Go DAWGS! Notice C. Beall running in front of the team.

Curtis and the UGA mascot, Hairy Dawg.

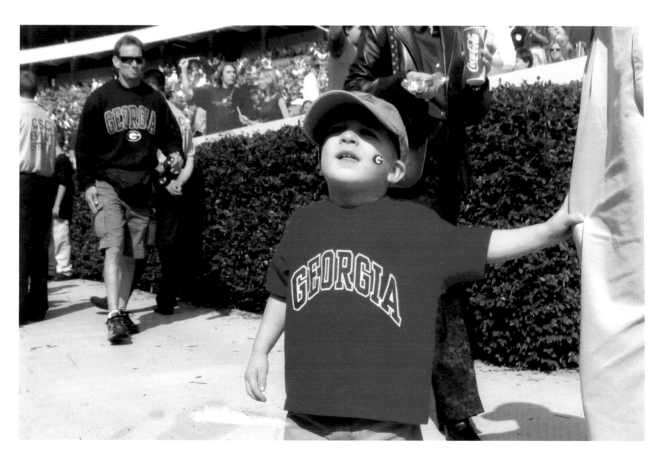

Following the family tradition, Tyler Chappell, C. Beall's great-grandson.

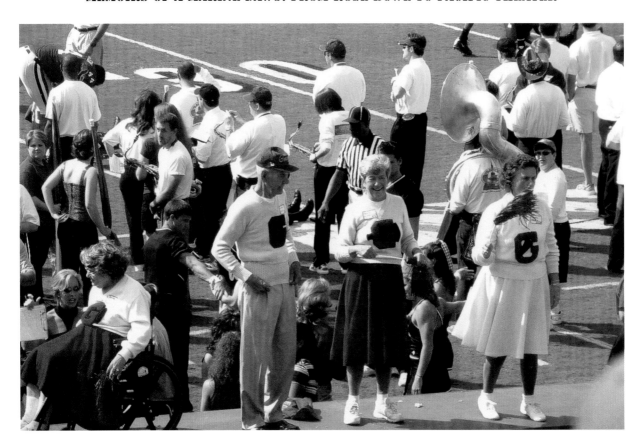

Above and below: Alumni cheerleaders are among UGA's most enthusiastic promoters; they never give up, and they never get tired.

Homecoming 2005

(Left to right) Alumni cherleaders ***LeAnn Hallford, Carolyn Hesler, Tommy Wilkerson, Susan Holtzclaw, Elsa Hirsh, Curtis Beall,*** *and* ***Bill Dunaway*** *pause for the playing of the national anthem before the Homecoming game Saturday. The University welcomes back its former cheerleaders, complete with vintage garb, each year as part of the Homecoming festivities. Below, Curtis waves to a friend along the parade route.*

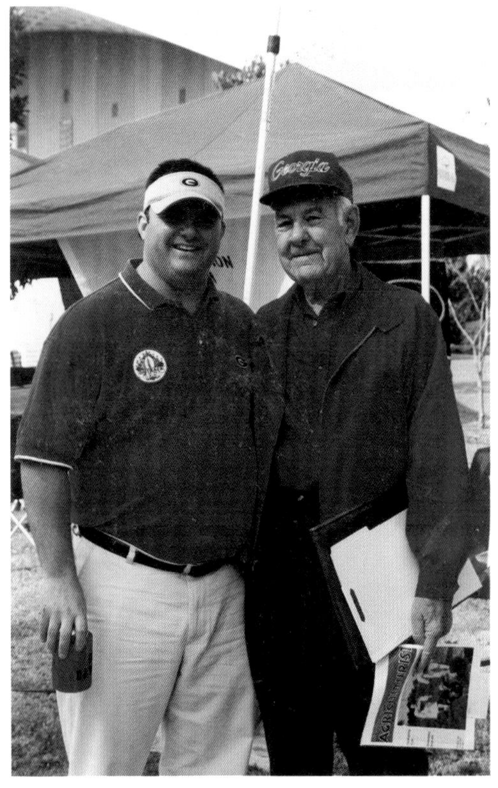

At left, Curtis Beall and Charlie Watts at the Georgia-Ole Miss game in November 2002.

Below, blue skies are a good sign on game day at Sanford Stadium.

Above: The whistle blows, ending the second quarter. Get ready for the half-time show!

UGA alumni cheerleaders enjoy their annual reunions; they are Bulldogs forever.

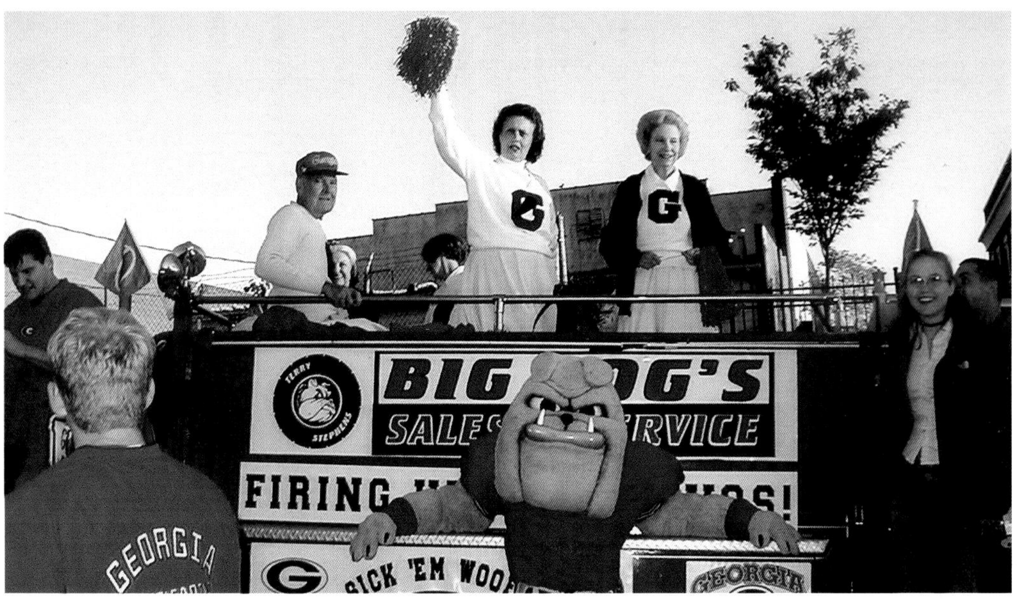

The Homecoming Parade is getting ready to roll. On the fire truck, left to right, are Curtis Beall, Dr. Bonnie Howard, and Louise Lidell.

Alumni cheerleaders Nancy Witherington, Dr. Bonnie Howard, and Curtis Beall celebrate UGA Homecoming with 90,000 of their close personal friends.

The half time show is about to begin; alumni cheerleaders can be seen on the field, in the left foreground.

Curtis Beall is in the center of everything when the Georgia Bulldogs play at Sanford Stadium.

On this Homecoming day, everybody cheers for Georgia. Curtis Beall, in red cap, center foreground, helps lead the cheers.

Curtis Beall and Jeff Lott (UGA "Mike-Man," 1991-94) at the 2002 Homecoming game in Athens. That's some stretch limousine!